Overcoming Writing Blocks

D0197250

J. P. Tarcher, Inc.
Los Angeles
Distributed by Houghton Mifflin Company
Boston

Overcoming Writing Blocks

By Karin Mack, Ph.D.
and
Eric Skjei, Ph.D.

Excerpts from *On Writing, Editing and Publishing* used by permission of Jacques Barzun. Quotations from *Conceptual Blockbusting, A Pleasurable Guide to Better Problem Solving* used with the permission of W.W. Norton & Company, Inc. Copyright © 1974, 1976 by James L. Adams.

Copyright © 1979 by Karin Mack, Ph.D. and Eric Skjei, Ph.D.

All rights reserved.

Library of Congress Catalog Card No.: 78-55592

ISBN: 0-87477-159-5

Design: Barbara Monahan
Art direction: John Brogna

Manufactured in the United States of America

Published by J. P. Tarcher, Inc.
9110 Sunset Blvd., Los Angeles, Calif. 90069

Q 10 9 8 7 6 5 4
First Edition

For

Alan and Deena
— K.M.

and

Gerhard Loepitz
— E.S.

You don't know what it is to stay a whole day with your head in your hands trying to squeeze your unfortunate brain so as to find a word.

— GUSTAVE FLAUBERT

Contents

Acknowledgments

We owe an immeasurable debt to all our students, friends, and clients, whose blocking and unblocking experiences created both the need and the basic material for this work. We also deeply appreciate the generous comments of Irene Bagge, Jacques Barzun, Norman Corwin, Judy Krantz, Nancy Kuriloff, Al Martinez, Paul Pierce, Frederick Pohl, Robert Reis, Sid Stebel, and Irving Wallace on the pleasure and pain of writing. Special thanks go to Nancy Kuriloff, for her work in the field.

But most of all, we especially want to thank Victoria Pasternack, our editor, whose unflagging encouragement and adroit direction are themselves unblocking aids any writer would be lucky to have.

How to Use This Book

Overcoming Writing Blocks is designed as a resource handbook, one that can be read through once or twice carefully, then used as individual discretion and need dictate. It is divided into three major sections. Part 1 is introductory. In it we define writing blocks, discuss the nature of blocking during the writing process, and point out what emotional and environmental influences contribute to causing writing blocks. Part 2 breaks the writing process into four overlapping stages and discusses the types of blocks common to each stage. Then, within the context of the separate stages, we present more than fifty unblocking techniques, illustrated by examples, anecdotes, and quotations from writers, critics, educators, and psychologists—all related to their experiences with writing blocks and the writing process. Part 3 presents case histories showing how the techniques may be applied to characteristic problems in four broad writing fields: business writing, student writing, technical/ academic/professional writing, and personal writing.

We introduce the unblocking techniques in a linear,

systematic way, arranging them along a continuum that parallels our view of the sequential stages of the writing process. This doesn't mean, however, that you should feel any sense of restriction. That is, as you read through the book and experiment with various techniques, if you find a particular unblocking technique that helps you unblock when you're first getting started, but we've placed it near the final stage of the writing process, you should feel free to use it whenever it is helpful to you. We are presenting no rigid formulas or rules for writing. The only rule is to use what works.

Part 1

*Understanding
Writing Blocks*

1

Blocking: What It Is

EARLY everyone who writes, even if only to draft a short business letter or dash off a personal note now and then, sooner or later comes up against a writing block. When you're blocked, the feeling is all too familiar. You're paralyzed. You feel panicky, terrified, your mind is a blank. You put a fresh page in the typewriter, you type a title or a salutation or your name at the top, and then you freeze. Nothing happens. Zero. Zilch.

This is blocking at its worst. Yet there are other, less severe, but also highly irritating indications that you're suffering from a writing block. You may not stop writing entirely, but the process will be slow and painful. You may eventually finish the job, but if you find yourself looking back on it with dread, with the sense that it was unnecessarily labored and halting, that you agonized over the piece much more than you needed to, then you've suffered some degree of blockage in the writing process.

A writing block is, quite simply, an obstacle to the free expression of ideas on paper. Somewhere between the thought and the recording of it there is an interruption in the flow. In *Overcoming Writing Blocks* you will learn to recognize this interruption and resume the flow. This book will show you how to sidestep, surmount, bypass, and in some cases learn to live peaceably with these obstacles to your free written expression.

As working writers, teachers of writing, and writing consultants ourselves, we have worked closely with scores of individuals from a spectrum of occupations—among them, students, teachers, salespeople, managers, accountants, ad agency executives, doctors, engineers, publicists, budding novelists, physicists, lawyers—who experience trouble with blocking. Whether they write only occasionally or every day, whether they write for a living, for professional distinction and advancement, or from purely personal motivations—writing blocks are familiar afflictions to them all.

In the process of helping them in workshops and private sessions, we have developed the extensive series of unblocking techniques that we set forth in this book. The techniques work. They work for blocking at the start of the process, when you can't seem to get yourself to sit down and think about the writing you have to do; they work to help you organize your raw material into a coherent whole; they work to get you started on writing rough drafts and to keep you at the process of putting words on the page; and they make the last phase of a writing task, revising and polishing, both possible and palatable.

Overcoming Writing Blocks is the distillation of our combined experience. It is a book for anyone who writes and has trouble doing so. Our focus is on the problem of blocking in writing that is intended to convey information. It is designed as a resource handbook to be read through at least once, then used as needed to cure your blocking symptoms.

Please note that this is not intended to be a book about style, which to us means putting the right words in the right places. Nor is this a book about the mechanics of writing or about the highly specialized prose used in any particular profession, field, or discipline—there are numerous good books on these subjects and we've listed some of them in the bibliography. Finally, although this is also not a book about fiction writing, which involves unique problems of characterization, plot, and dialogue, we have found that a writing block is a writing block, no matter what the written form, and a good many of our unblocking techniques are applicable to all forms of writing, including fiction.

If you keep only one thing in mind as you read on, remember that blocking is common, natural, and certainly not hopeless. It happens to nearly everyone, as our quotes and stories will show. But there are many effective, easily applied ways to extricate yourself from its snare, and we have collected for you here the best that we have encountered over the years from contacts with hundreds of writers.

You will find, as you read through the book, that you're already familiar with some of these methods, and that you may have actually used them before but were never quite fully aware of just what you were doing. Other methods, we hope, will seem new and ingenious to you. And one, or more, will work.

RECOGNIZING THE SYMPTOMS OF A WRITING BLOCK

Among the most obvious symptoms of blocking is procrastination. If you've got a writing job to do and you're blocking, you find yourself frantically looking for anything you can possibly find or contrive to distract yourself so that you can avoid having to get to work. You actively seek out diversions, one after another—trivial phone calls, lists of things to do next week, *alphabetized* lists of things to do next week, unnecessary conversations with co-workers, day-old newspapers you ordinarily wouldn't take the faintest notice of, and so forth. You smoke too much, drink too much coffee, and

> *"As I look back on it, I can see that my usual strategy has been to go over to the tailor's and have a suit made. The amount of time you can eat up simply by going through swatch booklets to choose a fabric . . . really gets the job done. After that you have at least three long fitting sessions to look forward to, plus intermediary trips to talk about darts, buttons, stepcollars, and American Bemberg linings."*
>
> — TOM WOLFE

nibble snacks compulsively—anything to keep from sitting down at your desk and working.

As your deadline creeps closer and closer, you feel helpless, stuck. You just can't seem to break through the impasse. Desperation makes you begin to plot wildly impractical escapes, like contracting Dengue fever, dropping the typewriter out the window, or catching the next flight to Rio. (We know one writer who got so panicked by an imminent deadline that he set fire to his apartment to avoid it.)

Blocking feels awful. You're stopped cold, dead in your verbal tracks, and you're convinced you'll never get started again. Your brain seems to have turned to oatmeal; you're groggy, indecisive, unfocused. You feel trapped. The walls are closing in. You're tense, irritable, angry. People around you look stupid and ugly. Your palms sweat. You feel dizzy, nauseous, restless.

And it's a vicious circle, because blocking feeds itself and infects everything else in your life. Feeling irritable, you snap at colleagues, friends, and family. They feel hurt and you feel guilty, all of which contributes to your irritation and your block. Because you're in a mental daze, time seems to pass with excruciating slowness; but when you look back on a day of being blocked, it seems to have flashed past, and the realization that your time is running out makes you feel even more depressed and fearful. The less productive you are, the more resentful you become about other demands made on your time, and the more overwhelmed and intimidated you feel by the need to master the topic and the material. There you sit, in dumb agony, with sharpened pencils, silent typewriter, and empty pages all staring blankly back at you.

Does that sound familiar? It's a bleak picture, but by no means a hopeless one. There are ways to cope with and master blocking, and we describe them in detail in this book. We also show how they can be applied to a number of typical blocking situations drawn from business, student, technical/academic/professional and private writing examples. But first, before we move on to the causes of writing blocks, let's look at a few scenarios that show some typical writing situations and the blocks that result. You are likely to recognize yourself in more than one of these portraits.

SOME WRITERS YOU'VE MET BEFORE

Bill T. needs to write a letter to a prospective customer, an important one, who is balking at the price of the line of computer products Bill represents. Bill is a well-prepared, dynamic, forceful salesperson in face-to-face meetings, but he agonizes when he has to write. Talking to someone is his strong suit; putting his thoughts on paper leaves him cold, mostly because he misses the immediate and personal feedback that speaking directly to another person involves. This time, though, Bill's prospect wants to see the prices and the reasons why he should buy from Bill—and he wants this information in writing.

Instead of working to pull a letter together, Bill blocks. He puts it off and puts it off, knowing that the longer he waits, the less likely the sale becomes. And his procrastination affects the rest of his work, since he can't get his mind off the letter he isn't writing. He feels preoccupied, guilty, and it intrudes into his other calls. Even when he's chatting with other people in his office, something keeps reminding him that he's refusing to come to grips with a basic problem.

Finally he hands some rough notes to one of the firm's trainees and vaguely asks if she would mind pulling them together into a letter. When the letter comes back across his desk for his signature, he can't bring himself to read it to see whether it's accurate and how it sounds. He knows that if he could just come to terms with his resistance to writing, he'd be much more effective at his job.

Jim J. has just completed a series of tests on a new steering mechanism he designed for the small planes that his company manufactures. His studies show that the device will ease handling, improve maneuverability, and make the firm's planes much safer—all of which are new features that the company wants to highlight in an ad campaign aimed at corporate executives.

The sales manager, delighted with Jim's work, has asked him to write up a graphic, punchy report on the new mechanisms for the field reps in her division. Jim is flattered, but as he sits down at his desk and looks at the stacks of charts, graphs, calculations, and computer printouts that litter his office, his heart sinks. How, he wonders, is he ever going to pull out the essential information, simplify it so it can be easily understood by a lay person, and then arrange it in a clear, logical, but comprehensive narrative?

Thinking about this assignment makes him feel sick. Jim has never regarded himself as a writer, and he's gotten used to communicating only in numbers and terms that fellow technical professionals can follow. A week goes by, then another. Jim would like to share his problem with someone, but he's too embarrassed to confess that he's blocked. The sales manager is beginning to get impatient, since the ad campaign is breaking soon, and she wants her people to be prepared to sell. Pointed memos from her show up on Jim's desk every day now.

Finally, in desperation, Jim puts in an all-night stint, amassing a pile of his best illustrations and loosely stringing them together with a sentence or two here and there. He submits the report on a Friday and goes home exhausted, with the uncomfortable suspicion that he's going to find it back on his desk for revision by Monday.

Kristy M. squirms uneasily in her seat as her history instructor passes out the essay topics for a midterm exam. She's been studying for this test for days, but now that she has the questions in hand, she's so tense that she can't even seem to read through the questions and understand what they're saying. As for preparing answers, she hasn't the faintest notion where to begin. She makes a few notes on her scratch paper, but they seem irrelevant, so she crosses them out. Her stomach feels tight. Her neck and shoulders ache. Her head is beginning to throb. Her thoughts keep jumping crazily from one unrelated topic to another.

As the minutes tick inexorably by, Kristy feels small, lost, and hopeless. The hour ends. She can barely bring herself to stand up, walk to the front of the room, and drop her blank test booklet on the teacher's desk. She feels utterly humiliated and defeated.

Susan N. teaches an experimental high-school-level math class. She enjoys her work, is an excellent teacher, and is well liked by her students and colleagues. But now she has a problem. The fiscal year is ending for the school district; the voters have mandated a reduction in educational funding for the coming year, and the school board is trying to decide where to cut back. Susan's master teacher, buried under a mountain of paperwork, has asked her to write up a summary evaluation on her class, to be used by the board in determining whether it should be continued.

Susan can't help but feel intimidated by the significance of the report. Her job is on the line and the pressure makes her anxious and hesitant. Because she wants to impress the board members, most of whom have years of teaching experience and advanced degrees, Susan tries to make her report sound impressive. She knows what she wants to say and would have less trouble putting it down in plain English, but she's afraid that she wouldn't make the right impression. Instead she falls back on the inflated educational jargon she was exposed to in college.

Halfway through the first draft, something inside Susan rebels and she finds she can't go on. When she sits down at her desk to work, all she feels is disgust and a terrible weariness. What she'd really like to do is tear the whole thing up and send the board a blistering letter, telling them just how fed up she feels at this uncalled-for harassment. She does her job and does it well. Why should she have to give them any more justification than that for keeping her on?

Sent out of town on an extended business trip by his firm, Brad N. struggles to express his feelings in letters to the woman he's been dating steadily for the past few months. He wants to let her know how much he misses her and how important she's become to him, but somehow he always winds up crumpling up his drafts and throwing them in the wastebasket. Writing about his emotions makes him feel foolish and weak. So instead he sends her a stream of post-cards covered with safe, trite notes about restaurants, business, and the weather, all the while hoping she will guess how he really feels about her.

Peter A. chokes on his toast as his eyes catch yet another article about a grisly murder in the morning paper. Outraged by what he considers to be a wildly hypocritical stand on the part of the publishers, who profess law and order but capitalize on crime by their lurid news coverage, Peter vows to write a caustic letter to the editor.

But every time he sits down to write, he loses his fire. Somehow Peter doesn't quite believe that he will be able to make his point as convincingly as the paper's experienced professional writers are able to make theirs. And this invidious comparison has the effect of making him feel incapable of sitting down and actually working through a draft. Instead, Peter continues to have nightmares about crime in the streets and to exasperate his friends by ranting on at every opportunity about the paper's duplicitous editorial policy.

Marilyn B. happily agreed to handle publicity for her daughter's school carnival but then had second thoughts when the carnival committee asked her to write up a short promotional piece on the upcoming event for the local newspaper. She hasn't done any writing since high school, and even then she remembers that she never felt secure in English classes. Although she has all the information about the carnival that she needs, Marilyn is afraid that her misspellings, shaky grammar, and what she's sure are trite phrases will make her and the school look foolish and dull.

Marilyn blocks unconsciously. Instead of sitting down and trying to take notes, make a list, work out an outline, and write a draft, she lets other obligations crowd writing out of her day. She does the laundry, runs errands, cooks dinner, makes telephone calls, and visits with her neighbors, telling herself that if she just had some free time, she could get that news item out of the way.

None of these blocked writers is simply apathetic or bored with the task. The antidote to that kind of inertia would be self-discipline . . . nothing more elaborate than just pulling up their socks and forging ahead. But mere self-discipline rarely works with a genuinely blocked writer, whose difficulty has recognizable emotional symptoms and some distinct psychological causes. In its severest forms, blocking makes writers feel not only anxiety-ridden, but also profoundly convinced that their generative power is gone for good, that they will never again be able to put two accurate, intriguing words together. And whatever self-confidence was there is, at least temporarily, at its lowest ebb.

What is responsible for these feelings? In the next chapter we'll take a look at what we believe to be the fundamental causes of blocking, since understanding the basis of your writing block is the first step in finding its cure.

2

Blocking: Why It Happens

UR combined experiences with people who must write—and who suffer when they do so—have shown us that there are generally three interdependent reasons for blocking at a writing task: (1) the fact that writing is hard work, (2) the fact that when you write you invite judgment by others — often critical — of your style, thoughts, and, by extension, yourself, and (3) the fact that when you write you evoke your own powerful chorus of internal critics, whom you developed long ago in an effort to anticipate criticism and thus spare yourself the pain of feeling foolish. These problems are directly related to the character and psychology of writing as a creative process.

WRITING AND THINKING ARE HARD WORK

Oddly enough, even some of the pros, writers who *have* to write because that's how they put bread on the table, share a common misconception about writing: They think their words should flow perfectly from opening sentence to conclusion in final, polished form on the first try.

25

Perhaps that's how it *should* be, ideally, but that's not how it is. No one, not even the professional, sits down and sets forth every word on the page exactly as it will appear in the finished version. All writing is the result of *rewriting*. And then more rewriting. It is never simple, direct dictation by the mind to the hand to the page. Instead it is a trial-and-error process of experimentation—more like a spiral than a straight line—a creative, exploratory interplay between the writer's goal, his stream of thoughts, and his responses to the words on the page. It's a lot of hard work.

"Let's face it, writing is hell."

— WILLIAM STYRON

Even when it's going superbly, the writing process is one of deliberate, often tedious labor, not only of forming the letters on the page, of pushing the pen or pounding the typewriter, but especially of the intense mental labor of sustained, focused concentration and the slow, fitful accumulation of letters, words, phrases, sentences, paragraphs, and pages. Rarely does that exhilarating moment or two of smooth, sure composition occur, when the writer's brain, hand, and eye move together in eloquent harmony, as if guided by the Muse herself.

"How do I know what I think until I see what I say?"

— E. M. FORSTER

Furthermore, smooth writing requires smooth thinking, and that's never easy even under the best of circumstances. The mental work that goes into writing—whether the task is a note on a get-well card, an office memo, or a history essay exam—involves constant discovery and rediscovery of what you're really trying to say. When you write, you're always evolving your thoughts, developing your point of view, and refining your choice of words as the process unfolds. The stuff of your thoughts and feelings is always somewhat nebulous until it begins to take shape in words on the page. And only when you've externalized it in writing can you see how it isn't quite right yet and how it must change to reflect what's going on inside your head. In thinking about writing you progress through a series of distinct mental stages, from first raw thought to ultimate separation from the polished final draft, and throughout the entire process you're constantly trying to translate psychological impressions into cold, hard print.

"Writing, like life itself, is a voyage of discovery."

— HENRY MILLER

A simple memo or a lengthy report offer the same challenge to the thinking-writing process. You take some notes, make a list or two, then, if you're not too blocked, launch into a rough draft. But no sooner do you have a paragraph or two down on the page than you begin to see that your first reflections weren't quite on target. That isn't *quite* what you thought you were trying to say. And suddenly, there you are in the middle of the quest for the best possible representation of your thoughts. Or you look ahead and see a new line of thought appearing that could reshape the work in a better way. You see how each added word, like a stone tossed into a still pool, sends out ripple after ripple, each merging with and altering the others.

"I never knew in the morning how the day was going to develop. I was like a hunter, hoping to catch sight of a rabbit."

— E. B. WHITE

Previous verbal patterns shift, disintegrate, then reform into something quite new and different, but still composed of the same basic elements. So you realign your thinking, and your writing, and you start over. (Or, if the critical feeling gets too strong, and you begin to feel that what's appearing on the page isn't quite right enough or good enough, you falter and stop dead in your tracks.) The chase can be exhilarating or stupefying, but it's never easy.

Zigzagging like this from creation to criticism and back again is often extremely frustrating, especially if you magnify it by feeling guilty about not being able to put down perfect words in perfect order the first time around. Those who aren't used to the process (and even those who are) often find themselves terribly upset by the feeling that they're wandering aimlessly around on the page. A deceptively small internal voice, which we will take a closer look at soon, keeps wondering why the writer seems so ambivalent: "Don't you know what you think?" it whispers. "C'mon, just get it out, stop being so hesitant, so indecisive, so weak!"

This experience of constantly discovering new possibilities, alternate ways to proceed, fresh ways to restructure and recast what you've written, rich as it may sound, can induce confusion, fear, and, eventually, blocking of the writer's decision-making faculties. This is especially true because there's never enough time to thoroughly explore all the possible permutations of the work. Deadlines are always nipping at the writer's heels. She can't really afford to indulge in endless speculation and experimentation. Decisions must be made, and they must be made *now*. So there can arise a paralyzing conflict between the need to understand the alternatives and the equally powerful need to bring the task to an end.

It takes energy and self-control to do all this. You have to be able to concentrate, to form your thoughts, to pick those that are central to the topic and reject those that aren't. And you have to be able to articulate them, to name them with sufficient accuracy and lucidity that someone else will know what you're talking about. There's no easy way to do this. But there are dozens of effective techniques for undercutting the fear and helping yourself out of the confusion that may stump you during the writing process. First, though, let's deal with the other psychological components of writing blocks.

WRITING IS VULNERABILITY

The fact that writing is hard, ambiguous, highly provisional work is by no means the most serious cause of blocking. A more powerful problem is the writer's own resistance to the self-exposure that writing inevitably entails.

Self-exposure comes about in the following way: When we write we want the reader to see things our way, to think in a special fashion about our subject, to see the topic in a certain light, or even to behave in a very specific manner—to buy this brand rather than that, to adjust the machine by turning this bolt not that, to see the firm from this perspective rather than that. We want, in short, to be persuasive.

And we are afraid that our most carefully crafted opinions will fall on deaf ears, that we'll be ignored or even repudiated and rejected. We fear that if we make the wrong choices, then instead of being heard, appreciated, and admired, we will evoke criticism. Instead of convincing, we will alienate—we will lose the respect and confidence of our readers, possibly even their love.

> *"I have discovered quite recently that the characteristic Freudian resistance to confessions of any sort, which are very well represented in all the writing blocks one goes through—the dizzy fits, the nauseas, and so on, and so forth, which almost every writer has recorded—are a standard pattern for all kinds of creative things."*
>
> — LAWRENCE DURRELL

Because we either consciously or unconsciously seek acceptance when we write, we make ourselves vulnerable. Writing is risky: It exposes us without our normal social defenses to criticism, to disagreement, to the possibility of failure. Once the deadline has passed and we're committed to print, we can't go back to explain what we "really" meant, as we can in conversation. Speech can be retracted, modified, and embellished by tone of voice, gesture, or facial expression. When we speak we can gauge the effect of our words on the listener. From this immediate feedback we can adjust our words as we wish.

Not so with writing. Once words are on the page they have an independent, more-or-less permanent existence. By committing himself to an idea, an opinion, or a particular choice of words, the writer has invested part of himself in what he's written. And this responsibility, this sense of self-exposure, can be paralyzing—especially because most of us have learned to equate how people respond to our writing with what they think of us. We come to identify with what we put on the page, to an extreme. "If I write poorly, woodenly, ungrammatically," we tell ourselves, "others will think of me critically, as an inferior, and I will be humiliated and embarrassed."

Justly or unjustly, most of us tend to think, "I *am* what I write" and I *am* how I write." We know whoever we're writing for will be responding not only to *what* we say, but also to *how* we say it—and as a consequence, we think, to what kind of human being we seem to be. They will skeptically analyze not only what we propose to tell them, but also who we are to make this claim on them, and why we should be heard. In short, we're on the spot. We've asked them to read us . . . now we have to deliver.

WRITING AND THE INTERNAL CRITIC

The critics outside us, those we fear we'll find in the audience, are a fundamental cause of blocking. But they pale in comparison to an infinitely more threatening voice of censure, that of the critic within us. This is the most powerful and most common cause of writing blocks: the suppressive, censorious voice of the internal critic.

All of us, through lifelong exposure to the well-meant

"The reason for your complaint [about not being creative] lies, it seems to me, in the constraint which your intellect imposes upon your imagination . . . . Apparently, it is not good—and indeed it hinders the creative work of the mind—if the intellect examines too closely the ideas pouring in, as it were, at the gates . . . . In the case of a creative mind, it seems to me, the intellect has withdrawn its watchers from the gates, and the ideas rush in pell-mell, and only then does it review and inspect the multitude. You worthy critics, or whatever you may call yourselves, are ashamed or afraid of the momentary and passing madness which is found in all real creators, the longer or shorter duration of which distinguishes the thinking artist from the dreamer. Hence you complain of unfruitfulness, for you reject too soon and discriminate too severely."

— FRIEDRICH SCHILLER

---

but inhibiting criticisms of parents, teachers, and, in later life, bosses, colleagues, and a host of other authority figures, have internalized a critical chorus, composed of all the nagging voices that have since childhood tried to impose perfectionist standards of achievement on us.

SOURCES OF THE CRITICAL VOICES

Why is this critical voice so powerful when we write? Think for a moment about the differences between the way we learn to speak and the way we learn to write. As toddlers, we were surrounded by people who applauded our efforts to talk. No matter how badly we garbled the simplest words, doting relatives praised our efforts. We were allowed to develop at more or less our own pace, and we were given strong positive reinforcement for each achievement. (By contrast, when this nurturing environment doesn't exist and a child is harshly corrected every time he fails to speak with perfect enunciation and clarity, he may develop a stutter or refuse to talk at all.)

Writing, however, isn't learned in a supportive, tolerant atmosphere. Consider this unfortunate but rather common early childhood experience. A youngster wants to write a story. She asks her teacher to help her. The teacher watches her write the first sentence, and then immediately interrupts the creative process to correct her spelling and syntax, and to point out errors of logic in the narrative. The child has asked for encouragement, not criticism, but in trying to be expressive and creative, she has met with judgment, correction, and redirection. The next time she feels the impulse to express herself, it will be overshadowed by her memory of the teacher's critical remarks. Eventually, after enough exposure to this kind of experience, she will internalize this critical voice and interrupt her own process of self-expression, slowly losing her receptivity to the creative side of writing.

And as she progresses through school, this child will again and again be taught, as she waits nervously to find out how her latest essay has been graded, that her value in the classroom—that is, her teacher's admiration for her as an individual—is strongly dependent on how well she writes. "I'm a 'C' student—average, undistinguished, with nothing special about me."

In high school, she will meet Mrs. Grundy, the archetypal English teacher, stern and inflexible, standing at the head of the class, casting a pall in the student's heart as she labors to make certain that she doesn't split an infinitive, end a sentence with a preposition, or use *like* when she should have chosen *as*. And when her papers come back with bold red marks scrawled across them, she will feel rueful, pained, and not a little angry about the bruises to her self-esteem.

"Too many writing instructors put you down. They make you feel that if you can't be a Tolstoy or a Flaubert or a Balzac there's no point in trying."

— IRVING WALLACE

In defense, she will vow to avoid exposing herself to that kind of censure again because it feels so bad, and thus she will continue the process of building her own innate critic, one who can do Mrs. Grundy's job before she does, thus

---

"Over the years I've never learned not to overcriticize myself."

— AL MARTINEZ
Los Angeles Times *feature writer and screenwriter*

---

defusing the teacher's comments and sparing the student the distress of public humiliation—but in the process inhibiting her pleasure and even her ability to write.

To give her her due, Mrs. Grundy has a point (she may actually know what good writing is and have some ideas about how to achieve it) as do most of the real-life models that help form our internal critic. But the danger is that our expressive side, which seems to be more tender and sensitive than our critical faculties, can suffer permanent damage when it comes under the critical lash too early. We turn from being confident and assertive about our imaginative and inventive impulses to being shy and "spookable"; we turn from being daring to being conventional, compliant, and submissive. In fact, we may even get angry and frightened if we encounter a teacher who encourages us to be genuinely creative and expects us to take real risks in our writing. The rules that once inhibited us become a crutch. We can't do without them, and the occasional suggestion that we should is a threat.

"If we ask what is the literary impulse par excellence we are, I think, bound to say that it is a desire to pull together one's conscious self and project it into some tangible constructed thing made up of words and ideas. The written thing may serve ulterior ends, as in exposition or polemic, but its first intention is to transfer a part of our intellectual and emotional insides into an independent and self-sustaining outside. It follows that if we have any doubts about the strength, truth, or beauty of our insides, the doubt acts as an automatic censor which quietly forbids the act of exhibition."

— JACQUES BARZUN
Critic and educator

After we move beyond the classroom, the critic finds new reinforcement, in the form of bosses, colleagues, and other powerful individuals with whom we form close relationships. It becomes an entrenched part of our personality. We find ourselves, as adults, afraid to fail, afraid to take the risks inherent in learning. And because putting our thoughts down on paper is such an overt way of exposing ourselves to public scrutiny, and possibly criticism, the internal critic is particularly active and suppressive when we try to write. Unless we learn to recognize his voice, understand that he is often unnecessarily wary and defensive, and manage his inhibiting presence, we will constantly have trouble with blocking.

Managing the Critic

When you can hear him, the internal critic speaks in a shrill, querulous tone—rational, dour, often pessimistic and anxious, alert only to the dangers of the world around us and therefore to the shortcomings in our work. Assuming the voices of parents, teachers, and other authority figures, he whispers and sometimes shouts that our writing is bad. His often snide voice judges the quality and correctness of our prose. He comments on form, style, language, and organization. He edits words and thoughts before we have a chance to put them on paper, and thus creates blank-page panic. He rejects angles, intuitions, and conceptual frameworks before we have even a remote chance to explore our alternatives. Even if you can't actually hear his voice (or voices), you know that he's present when you're trying to write if:

- You feel you have to revise every line until it's just right before going on to the next one.

- You're ashamed of what you consider to be "bad writing" anywhere in the first draft, even though you know perfectly well that no one but you will ever see it.

- You let yourself get completely bogged down looking for the right word.

- You're afraid of seeming childish, overly enthusiastic, or too eager.

- You're afraid of sounding unintelligent, ungrammatical, or illiterate. You become obsessed by the mechanics of writing, rather than permitting yourself a free flow of expression.

- You write without emotion—you tend to be both bland and stuffy.

- You refuse to even consider discussing your work with anyone else until it's completely finished.

- You tend to believe that writing should be easier than it is for you, that somehow it's all your fault that you have to work so hard at it.

As you can see, the internal critic makes us feel stultified, boring, and stale. He completely fails to empathize with the writer's need to remain open to discovering the next level of meaning that always emerges from the draft. And he reinforces the delusion that our entire worth rides on the written line.

As well as being a critic, he is also an internal censor, one who inhibits the emotional content of our work. Like all censors, he is bigoted and narrow-minded, and his intolerance frustrates and blocks us further. To women he may insist that direct, forceful, flashy writing isn't "feminine," and so a business letter or firm recommendation turns into a meek plea or carefully hedged suggestion. Speaking to a man, he may say that expressions of emotion or doubt are weak and unprofessional, undermining the writer's ability to move his reader.

As we have said, the internal critic develops as a protective figure that enables us to anticipate and thus pre-empt the potentially harsh reactions of an impersonal, indifferent world. But when he causes writing blocks he exceeds his role and becomes a tyrant, forcing us to see our work in the light of impossible, perfectionistic standards.

What we have not yet said is that the judgments of the internal critic are constructive at the right time and place—but never during the early and middle phases of the writing process, when we're trying to feel our way through the concepts and get them down on the page in rough drafts. His presence can only be destructive at these stages. Yet in the final phase of the writing process, the revision stage, the critic does have a constructive role to play.

Dr. Desy Safán-Gerard, a psychotherapist and painter with extensive experience in treating blocking in the arts, put it this way in an article in *Psychology Today:* "The most disruptive quality of these internal critics is that they come into play before we need them. Evaluation should take place *after* expression." And James Adams, Stanford University professor of design and author of *Conceptual Blockbusting*, concurs:

> If one analyzes or judges too early in the problem-solving process, he will reject many ideas. This is detrimental for two reasons. First of all, newly formed ideas are fragile and imperfect—they need time to mature and acquire the detail needed to make them believable. Secondly, . . . ideas often lead to other ideas. Many techniques of conceptualization . . . depend for their effectiveness on maintaining "way-out" ideas long enough to let them mature and spawn other more realistic ideas. It is sometimes difficult to hold on to such ideas because people generally do not want to be suspected of harboring impractical thoughts. However, in conceptualization one should not judge too quickly.

The trick then, is to squelch the critic's intrusive, obnoxious voice in the early stages of the writing process and invite his contribution at the end. Otherwise, he will speak up just when we need the freest possible play of imagination and succeed in inhibiting creativity by making us feel self-conscious.

Jacques Barzun states in a note to us that he feels there may be more than one kind of critic:

> I do not think the critical mind of the writer who is revising is the same censor as the other; for it is notorious that No. 1, the negative, stops all action, whereas No. 2, the judicial, overlooks many errors and absurdities in a mood of complacent self-satisfaction. No. 1 inspires total fright and total silence. No. 2 is like a woman primping in front of her mirror. She may put in some good strokes, but she has a fundamentally favorable idea of herself.

However many critics there may be, the internal critic represents only a reactive side of you, not a generative, creative one. In the next chapter we will show you how to keep him from dominating your work to the point of bringing it to a halt, how to suppress his voice, and how to postpone paying attention to his nagging until the last stage, when his accumulated wisdom of rules and strategies can help you revise and polish your work.

In many ways, this book is about techniques for coping with his inhibiting presence through all stages of the writing process.

Part 2

The Writing Process and Unblocking Techniques

OOKING at the writing process as a whole—from first idea to cleanly typed finished product—often makes the task confronting you seem overwhelming, confusing, impossibly unwieldy. The key to overcoming this confusion is to break the process down into manageable parts—what we will identify as the stages of the writing process. Although we discuss these stages as sequential for the sake of clarity, it is important to recognize that no creative process ever flows smoothly from beginning to end. There is always much backtracking and jumping ahead along the way. In fact, this pattern is not only normal for the writer, it is also an effective way of unblocking.

Ease in writing comes from flexibility and trust in yourself, which comes from learning to tolerate a certain amount of chaos. It's entirely natural to feel confused and intimidated when you face any new writing task, whether it's a brief business letter or a mountain of technical information that has to be organized into effective publication. It is also inevitable that you'll begin with words that will need revision. And it's equally certain that you will find yourself resisting going back to change the text once you've managed to finally pull it all together into a complete draft.

Because writing is such an experimental process, it may help you to think of it as a spiral rather than a straight line. As though the writer were climbing a spiral staircase, he ascends by circling round and round, rising just a bit higher with each circuit, but constantly passing over the same ground—touching on the same basic topics, ideas, images, and phrases in search of their truest expression. However, as we have already indicated, the process can also be thought of in sequential stages, each representing a slightly further progression along the path from nebulous idea to finished draft.

The four stages we have distinguished correspond closely to what Dr. Safán-Gerard describes as the stages of any creative process: perception, elaboration, expression, and evaluation. She claims that these stages occur at every interaction with the work at hand, no matter where in the creative process you may be. That is, she considers the process a constantly repeating loop. For the sake of simplicity, however, we present the process in sequential stages, which we call: (1) preparing to write, (2) organizing your thoughts and material into an appropriate conceptual framework, (3) writing rough drafts, and (4) revising. Each of these stages has its characteristic blocking problems, as you probably already have discovered. However, don't let them discourage you. The more success you have in getting yourself to write easily—by using the techniques we present for each stage of the process—the more pleasurable writing will become for you and the less often you will find yourself blocking.

THE FOUR STAGES OF THE WRITING PROCESS

Part 2 of *Overcoming Writing Blocks* is divided into four chapters, each corresponding to one of the four stages of the writing process—preparing to write, organizing, writing rough drafts, and revising—each containing a discussion of the unblocking techniques most appropriate for use in managing difficulties that tend to arise at that stage.

The first stage, called prewriting, is an incubation stage. More than anything else, your job as a writer at this stage is to cultivate a special quality of receptivity to make

---

"One must allow the unconscious to struggle with problems. Incubation is important in problem-solving. It is poor planning not to allow adequate time for incubation in the solution of an important problem."

— JAMES ADAMS

---

yourself as sensitive as possible to faint suggestions about the work that crop up in the back of your mind. Once you know what your task is, you begin to explore it, gathering information, trying out different leads, and generally seeking to encourage the texture of the piece to take clearer and clearer shape in your mind and in your notes.

The emphasis in this stage of the writing process is on ways to approach your project with a maximum of creative freedom and a minimum of anxiety. This stage also involves learning how to take active control over the writing environment so as to eliminate distractions, how to schedule large jobs into bite-size units, and how to practice deliberate, systematic relaxation of the mind and body. Chapter 3 treats the role of the internal critic in more detail and outlines ways to squelch his inhibiting voice during this idea-gathering phase of your writing task.

The second stage of writing is almost purely organizational. It begins when there's enough material at hand so that you can begin to arrange it in the order that most accurately reflects the best natural structure for the concepts you're dealing with. This is a problematic task. A common complaint among the block sufferers we've talked to is that they can't seem to figure out where to start because they feel overwhelmed by the sheer quantity of information, examples, anecdotes, ideas, and perspectives, all of which seem equally significant. In Chapter 4, we describe different techniques designed to help the blocked writer see more clearly which aspects of a topic are primary and central and which are secondary and supportive. We show you how to list points, try loose outlines, and maintain a clear and constant focus on your purpose and your audience.

Up to this point in the process, the writer has prepared by collecting thoughts and ideas and has begun to pull the scattered pieces into a coherent—though still open-ended—framework. In very short pieces of writing, these first two stages—preparation and organization—may take up only a few minutes. If the writer is not blocking, they may be compressed into a quick blur of insight that inspires, informs, and organizes all at once. In longer pieces, the writer may take weeks or months to work through these stages and the blocking they can cause.

Now, at the third stage, which is discussed in Chapter 5, the writer is ready to begin actually writing a rough draft. The goal—and the source of the most common blocking problem—is simply to put pen to paper, get the words to start flowing, and then keep them coming once the draft is under way. It may seem that this third stage should proceed smoothly because the information is there and the organizational road map tells the writer approximately where each piece of it should go. The writer can now relax and let the words fill the page. Unfortunately, this is often not the case. Confronted with the need to create coherent, informative sentences, the writer often becomes most seriously intimidated by the task at this point.

Some of our techniques to unblock you at this stage, such as the Sensory Monologue, take you back to basics: You resort to describing only what you can see, smell, hear, and touch in the immediate surroundings. Others depend on recognizing that your thoughts are an ever-flowing stream; all you have to do is dip into them to find something to put on the page. Your thoughts may not seem directly pertinent to your topic, but we show you how this pertinence can then be developed. We also point out the value of images, memories, and daydreams as starting points for a draft.

To keep you writing, we suggest ways to bring new vitality to the process when you feel yourself faltering partway through—by changing the tools you use, by changing your authorial personality, or by playfully changing the style of the piece itself. And for writers who must work on more than one project at a time, we discuss creatively juggling the projects to relieve tension, so that each project gets your best effort.

The fourth stage is revision. This is often difficult for writers to reconcile themselves to; having endured the trauma of the birth of the work, the demand to go back and reshape it can be intolerable. The temptation to call it quits and throw up your weary hands at the end of the first draft can be irresistible. But as we can't say too often, everyone who writes learns at some point that all writing is rewriting, until the work is as good as time and talent can make it.

To help the blocked writer overcome the dread of revising, we set forth a number of procedures in Chapter 6, most of which fall into two categories: (1) those devoted to helping the writer develop detachment and objectivity by setting the work aside for a while and then coming back to it, by reading it out loud, and by paraphrasing it to a friend; and (2) those that involve inviting the internal critic to step in now and become actively involved in the rewriting process to make use of his judgmental skills—those same critical perspectives that only caused problems earlier in the process. Here we also provide a brief overview of certain mechanical tools of revising and copy editing that everyone who writes must have at least a nodding acquaintance with.

Every writer and every piece of writing, no matter how short or long, how simple or complex, passes through something resembling the process we've described, and often does so more than once. Whether the stages are sharply compressed, combined, or experienced in another sequence, they are always present. For instance, the writer may hit on the best way to organize the text while still gathering ideas, or revise the outline in the second stage of the process, and, feeling a mental kaleidoscope shift, suddenly realize that he or she has to go back to the original premises and start all over again from a more accurate perspective. All of this is to be expected. Feel free to move from stage to stage whenever you find yourself bogging down.

And please note that because the stages of the writing process have been set forth here in a linear fashion doesn't mean that our descriptions of unblocking techniques for these stages must be followed in the same way. Read through this part of the book, then study the stages or stage where you most often find yourself having trouble. Try various techniques until you find those that work best for you. Where you block and which techniques will work best to help you unblock will change, from day to day, from job to job, so keep on experimenting.

3

Preparing to Write

THIS is a training and gestation stage of any writing task: You know what you have to do and, overwhelmed as you may feel, you must prepare yourself properly for it. Just as you would prepare yourself for a footrace, so you need to develop basic fitness habits that will get you in shape for prose composition, especially if you know you have a tendency to block.

The paramount symptom of blocking at this first stage is restless, anxious procrastination. You can think of a thousand things you'd rather be doing than sitting at your desk pushing your pen, and when you do finally force yourself to sit down, dozens of extraneous but apparently urgent

---

"I play patience, or draw marvelously intricate patterns on backs of old newspapers while I'm solving the crossword. Then I feel ashamed and try to get back to work, but the phone rings or Edith calls me to tea, so I put it off for a later day."

— J.R.R. TOLKIEN

---

thoughts bubble up, as your recalcitrant mind ingeniously struggles to distract itself from the task at hand. Then, when you do finally manage to focus your attention on the job, all you get is a dull blankness, or nothing but the most obvious, banal truisms. There's no excitement, no inspiration about the whole project; it leaves a flat, sour taste in your mouth.

So you must prepare—mentally, emotionally, and physically—for the work ahead. This can mean a few minutes of note-taking, relaxing, or maybe chatting with a friend in a neighboring office. It can mean wandering around for half an hour, sharpening pencils and brewing a fresh cup of tea. It can mean getting a couple of important calls out of the way, then leaning back and practicing a few simple muscle-relaxing exercises. It can mean taking a walk. Whatever you seem to be doing at this stage, if you're doing it right, you will actually be orienting yourself toward the writing—mulling it over, watching the seeds of possible leads, organizational patterns, and particularly apt phrasings blooming in your mind. If none of this is happening, if all you're feeling is resentment, panic, and obsessive distraction with trivia, you are blocking and you need some deliberate and methodical techniques to counter it.

This chapter groups unblocking techniques under four basic categories, which correspond to the four chief blocking problems encountered in the prewriting phase: managing the environment, reducing tension, coming up with ideas, and increasing motivation.

If you're having trouble with persistent distractions in your physical surroundings, we suggest ways to manage them better so as to create privacy and an environment more conducive to writing. Tension, of both the muscles and the mind, is a pervasive problem for blocked writers at all stages of the process, and we touch on a number of practical, systematic ways to cope with it. For writers experiencing a paralyzing lack of ideas, we set forth some simple, reliable ways to come up with a basic concept or line of thought to build the piece on. Finally we address the problem of in-adequate motivation, of a sheer lack of excitement about the writing. We describe ways to uncover your own emotional barriers to writing, ways to get a better sense of and more control over your internal critic, and we go over a few simple ways to introduce a new sense of excitement into the writing process.

As we take you through this series of tasks, you will begin to understand that it moves from the environmental to the physical to the conceptual and finally to the volitional. At the start of the process of unblocking, all you concentrate on is the most tangible aspects of your writing situation: arrang-ing your physical surroundings and relieving your tension. Then you gradually turn inward, working to articulate your thoughts and feelings about writing and about coping with the internal critic. Slowly you assume a more active, posi-tive, self-assertive attitude toward yourself and your work. Next you focus on the topic itself, setting up systems to catch the fragments of thought and fact that help begin and build the text. Finally you arrive at a point where you are not only ready but eager to begin.

MANAGING YOUR WRITING ENVIRONMENT

Creative concentration has the power to make your senses especially acute and abnormally sensitive to the slightest stimuli. When you're concentrating successfully, this heightened attention enhances your thoughts and the words flow onto the page smoothly and powerfully. When you're blocked, however, your attention perversely gravitates to-ward the slightest distraction in your environment. Your ears pick up the faintest sounds. Your eyes wander back to the tree branch tossing outside the window or the dust motes floating in the sunlight. Your thoughts are fragmented. Your sentences, if they appear at all, turn out soft, mushy, repeti-tive. You feel victimized by your inattentiveness, because you find yourself guiltily inviting interruptions, knowing that they give you a welcome break from the frustration of being stuck.

Speaking of "environmental blocks," James Adams, author of *Conceptual Blockbusting*, says:

> The most obvious blocks are the physical. Plainly the physical surroundings of the problem-solver influence his productivity. I am sure that all of you are familiar with the effect of distractions. It is very difficult to work on complicated problems with continual phone interruptions. At times even potential distractions are a problem since when one is in a frustrating phase of problem-solving he is quite tempted to take advantage of such opportunities. Personally speaking, when involved in problem-solving I will go to heroic efforts to be distracted. Often I have to force myself out of bed at an inhuman hour in the morning to work on a problem when I am sure I can find no alternative activities available and no one to talk to. Even then, I often just sit hoping that someone will wake up and distract me.

Sit back for a minute and think about where you usually try to write. Are you in the middle of a busy office, surrounded by typewriters clacking away and the constant ringing of phones? Do your co-workers continually interrupt you with questions, demands, reminders? Do your eyes keep jumping from the unfinished page to the stack of unanswered letters on the desk?

Or maybe you're trying to write in isolation, in your home, after everyone has left for school or office and the morning's errands are done, and you're finding that you can't seem to keep your mind on what you want to say. The very absence of purposeful domestic bustle preoccupies you when you sit down to write.

No matter what kind of writing you need to do, the first place to begin overcoming a block—your physical setting—

is also the most obvious and the easiest to change. By taking charge of your environment and rearranging it to promote comfort plus a minimum of distraction (or as much as your situation permits) you begin a process that also leads to taking charge of yourself and your writing. Just the simple feeling that you're actively molding your surroundings will dispel the helpless feeling that being blocked brings on and will carry over into the writing process as well. The energy needed to push desks and filing cabinets around is the same needed to execute the writing task at hand.

You can gain a clearer sense of what's wrong with your current setting by contrasting it with a fantasy of your ideal writing space. Take a minute or two, lean back, and indulge yourself. What would perfect writing conditions for you be like? A long table to spread your papers out on? A heavy roll-top desk? Plenty of natural light? A globe in one corner? Note the details carefully. Do you want a view, or are you happier without visual distractions? Are you seated? In what type of chair?

"It's very important to me to have space, desk space. I'm always cluttering it up and constantly fighting to get room on that big table, because there are so many things on it. I spread out . . . papers, books, notes . . ."

— NORMAN CORWIN
Network broadcast writer

Maybe you're a completely horizontal author, like Proust and Mark Twain, who preferred to write while lying in bed. Or maybe, like Thomas Wolfe and Hemingway, you feel best when you can write standing up.

In your ideal setting, are there other people around, or

are you entirely alone? Some writers need absolute privacy and total silence in order to create. Others, like Jane Austen, have worked best while seated in the middle of a family hubbub, or, like Isaac Asimov, with the radio blaring.

"I don't want to speak to anybody or see anybody. Perfect silence."

— KATHERINE ANNE PORTER

Do you find when you're blocked that you're especially sensitive to noise? It can't usually be entirely shut out, unless, à la Proust, you're willing to line the room with cork, but it can be countered with soft music, a white noise machine, or earplugs.

Your fantasy may not be readily attainable, particularly in a business setting, but working carefully and deliberately through this simple imagination exercise will point up some of the stronger contrasts between the way you'd like to work and the conditions under which you're working now. And you'll be surprised at how many small modifications you *can* make that will give you a more effective writing atmosphere. Even if you don't come up with a very distinct picture of the perfect writing space, just thinking in these terms will help move you from passively enduring your environment to actively doing something about it.

Since the point of this technique is to set your decision-making faculties in motion, your choices can actually be quite arbitrary, or even capricious, as long as they involve exerting active control over your writing conditions. Truman Capote, for example, manages his writing environment by imposing on it an extensive set of ritualistic prohibitions:

I have to add up all numbers: there are some people I

never telephone because their number adds up to an unlucky figure. Or I won't accept a hotel room for the same reason. I will not tolerate the presence of yellow roses—which is sad because they're my favorite flower. I can't allow three cigarette butts in the same ashtray. Won't travel on a plane with two nuns. Won't begin or end anything on a Friday. It's endless, the things I can't and won't. But I derive some curious comfort from obeying these primitive concepts.

The only rule you need to follow is to make yourself as comfortable as possible. Experiment with changes in your surroundings to see what works best for you. If you're office-bound, move your desk. Adjust your chair. Close the door. If you're free to come and go as you please, try taking a pad and pen to the park, the library, or the unused conference room. Whatever starts the creative juices flowing, even if it's contemplating a bust of Shakespeare, don't hesitate to try it out. What constitutes a good working environment is entirely a matter of individual taste.

Using Props

Every stage needs a few props. For writing, pick an article or two that symbolizes your commitment to yourself and your work. For example, try using a good pen that makes a smooth line, or different colors of ink. Look for something that feels good and will help keep the words flowing. Your paper may be important: Do you prefer lined or unlined, white or colored? Maybe you compose best at an electric typewriter with a variety of typing fonts. The possibilities are endless.

A picture of Strindberg hung on the wall over Ibsen's desk because he found that those "demon's" eyes gazing down on him acted like a powerful writing stimulant. Schiller liked to have the fragance of rotting apples fill the room where he worked. Samuel Butler needed a literal prop: a heavy copy of *Lives of Eminent Christians* that he used to support his writing board. (An editor we know has trouble working without her favorite coffee cup close by her right hand.)

Anything and everything can successfully function as a writing prop: a cartoon, a favorite quotation tacked to the wall, a poster on the door, a freshly cut flower, a porcelain tea cup, or just a ragged old sweatshirt and a pair of decrepit slippers actually adorning the writer at her desk.

Pulling Up the Drawbridge

It's one thing to pick up a favorite pen or push a desk and chair around to make your environment suit you better, but it's something else again to manage the most animate part of your surroundings: people—family, friends, and fellow workers—those who know you well and are interested in your company or fascinated by what you're doing. The closer they are to you, the harder it is to insist on taking the time to yourself that you must have without feeling selfish.

If you work in an office, don't hesitate to tell your co-workers that you don't want to be interrupted for a while when you need to write. Close the door. Have someone else take your calls. Tape up a "Do Not Disturb" sign.

"I have a sign on the door that says: DO NOT COME IN. DO NOT KNOCK. DO NOT SAY HELLO. DO NOT SAY 'I'M LEAVING.' DO NOT SAY ANYTHING UNLESS THE HOUSE IS ON FIRE . . . *Also, telephone's off!"*

— JUDY KRANTZ
Author of the best-selling novel, Scruples

If you work at home, explain to your friends and family that even though you're at home, you really *are at work* and you really *do* need to be left alone at certain times. Tell them you aren't available between 8:00 and 2:00, or 10:00 and 4:00. You may want to invest in a recording machine for the telephone so that its ringing doesn't disturb your concentration. Remember that it's up to you to make it clear to the rest of the world that you simply aren't available, even for the most well-meant invitations, during certain times.

"'It is only half-an-hour'—'It is only an afternoon'—'It is only an evening,' people say to me over and over again; but they don't know that it is impossible to command one's self sometimes to any stipulated and set disposal of five minutes—or that the mere consciousness of an engagement will sometimes worry a whole day. These are the penalties paid for writing books. Who ever is devoted to an art must be content to deliver himself up wholly to it, and to find his recompense in it. I am grieved if you suspect me of not wanting to see you, but I can't help it; I must go my way whether or no."

— CHARLES DICKENS

Make Firm Writing Appointments with Yourself

The most important part of managing your work environment is managing your time. Blocking makes you tend to let your writing responsibilities slip to the bottom of your priorities, since facing up to them is so unpleasant. The first step in regaining some control over the process is to designate a specific time for the job. If you know at 9:30 in the morning that you have a half-hour job that has to get done before the close of the business day, schedule a firm time slot for writing the rough draft, say 11:00 to 11:30. Then schedule a second time, say 2:30 to 3:00, when you can come back to it, after having set it aside for a while, to see if there's any way it can be polished. Making writing appointments like this won't in and of itself unblock you, but it's an invaluable first step toward building a more disciplined foundation for your writing. (See our bibliography for an excellent book on time management by Alan Lakein.)

If you have a long job to do, set aside a regular time interval each day for writing, then follow your schedule. Pick a time of the day to write when you are at your best. Physiological research shows that some people, called "larks," are at their brightest early in the day, but tend to fade as the day wears on. Others, the "owls," start out slow but come alive as evening approaches. Try to figure out, if you haven't already, which of these two categories fits you best, or whether you seem to function equally well at all times of the day.

"I prefer the morning now, and just for two or three hours. In the beginning I used to work after midnight until dawn, but that was in the very beginning. Even after I got to Paris I found it was much better working in the morning."

— HENRY MILLER

EATING AN ELEPHANT: ONE BITE AT A TIME

Starting a new writing task, especially a long one, often causes a feeling of desperation, of being overwhelmed by the quantity of the material, by the need to organize it, to find the proper expression for it. And this of course can bring on a severe block.

How does one manage this feeling of being overwhelmed? It's like eating an elephant: You do it one bite at a time. Sit down and spend a few minutes breaking the project into logical bite-size units. Check your deadline. If it's a big project, figure out how far along you want to be with the job by when. Then mark these stages down on your calendar.

On long jobs, the stages you select will often be natural divisions of the work itself: Introduction, Chapter I, Chapter II, and so on. An alternative way to sequence out your writing, however, is to set up a daily quota—so many pages per hour or day.

This is how Anthony Trollope, the most prolific English novelist of the nineteenth century, managed his writing process:

> When I have commenced a new book, I have always prepared a diary, divided into weeks, and carried it on for the period which I have allowed myself for the completion of the work. In this I have entered, day by day, the number of pages I have written, so that if at any time I have slipped into idleness for a day or two, the record of that idleness has been there, staring me in the face, and demanding of me increased labour, so that the deficiency might be supplied. According to the circumstance of the time—whether my other business might be then heavy or light, or whether the book which I was writing was or was not wanted with speed—I have allotted myself so many pages a week.

By breaking a lengthy, complex writing job into chewable pieces, you give yourself the freedom to concentrate on each step as you work with it. You can relax and give yourself over to the stage at hand because you have the reassurance of knowing that you've worked out a master plan first.

Once you've Made a Writing Appointment or established a schedule, stick to it. You may find now and then that you arrive at that appointed hour still very blocked and that all you can do is sit there, unable to work. Try not to let this distress you. As you experiment with other unblocking techniques, you'll find yourself more and more capable of writing on demand, and the ability to integrate a chunk of writing time into your other routines will become more natural. You will become more decisive and efficient, of necessity. And once the writing time is over, you'll be able to move on to other business without that leftover remorse that comes up when you postpone a job until that magical point when you "have time to do it."

LIMBERING UP AND PROGRAMMED DAWDLING

As you know all too well, the usual blocking struggle is to keep procrastination at bay, to recognize it before it can begin its insidious attack on you, and head it off before it can erode your energies.

There is a way to make your tendency to procrastinate work for you, rather than against you. Instead of battling to resist it, trick it into usefulness. Try deliberately inviting it into your writing schedule, planning for it but keeping a very tight rein on just how much dawdling you indulge in. Call it a warm-up, fit it in at the beginning of your writing period,

---

"I'll write letters, answer mail, get things off my mind before I start writing for the day."

— IRVING WALLACE

---

and spend it doing just those things that you customarily use to keep from having to sit down and put pen to paper. Get a cup of coffee. Sharpen your pencils. Make a phone call. Neaten your desk. Water the plants. Read the paper. Re- move your makeup. Polish the firewood. Wax the ceiling.

As you do these things, keep in mind that you're actually already beginning the writing process, you're limbering up, incubating ideas, clearing your throat before launching into eloquence. In the back of your mind, consider the issues that are coming up in your writing. Try out a phrase. Carry on a dialogue with your reader. Mentally run down the list of points you want to be sure to make. Keep a pen and pad of paper or a stack of index cards handy to record valuable additions, concepts, words, or sentence fragments that come along unexpectedly.

"After all, most writing is done away from the typewriter, away from the desk. I'd say it occurs in the quiet, silent moments, while you're walking or shaving or playing a game, or whatever, or even talking to someone you're not vitally interested in. You're working, your mind is working, on this problem in the back of your head."

— HENRY MILLER

Eventually, if you keep on making this association between warming up and preparing to write, you'll find that you've trained yourself to treat wandering around the office or house as a useful prelude to writing. (You may even find yourself impatiently cutting the warm-up short because you're so eager to get to work. This is fine. Go ahead and respond to the creative impulse whenever it appears by sitting down and going to work. Later, if you lose your head of steam, just program another dawdling session into your day. Get up and wander around again.)

Keep your dawdling under control. Give yourself 15 to 30 minutes and no more. As you know from your own experience, delays of any kind can mushroom from minutes to hours to days to weeks unless you watch them carefully.

SYSTEMATIC RELAXATION STRATEGIES

Blocked writers we've talked with agree that one of the worst problems with blocking anxieties is that they make you too physically and mentally tense to work well. Blocking makes your heart begin to race, your breathing become fast and shallow, your stomach tighten up. You get headaches. Your hands and feet get cold and clammy. Your thoughts become jumpy and superficial. You can't focus on the topic.

This is a stress reaction known as the "fight-or-flight" response. At an earlier stage in evolution, the human animal, when confronting a threat in the environment, would take action to preserve itself by fighting or by running away. In terms of blocking, fight-or-flight anxiety only leads to tension, which aggravates the block, in turn making the tension even worse. In other words, when you feel panicky and tense about writing, your emotional state triggers physiological changes that make you more jittery and further inhibit your ability to write.

"It is also important to be able to relax in the midst of problem-solving. One's overall compulsiveness is less fanatical when he is relaxed, and the mind is more likely to deal with seemingly "silly" combinations of thoughts. If one is never relaxed, his mind is usually on guard against non-serious activities, with resulting difficulties in the type of thinking necessary for fluent and flexible conceptualization."

— JAMES ADAMS

You can control this anxiety reflex by learning to reverse the process so that you work "from the outside in," starting with your tense muscles, systematically relaxing them, and then turning your attention to your racing mind and deliberately calming it too. Conscious mechanical tightening and then relaxing of your muscles sharply decreases body tension, heart rate, blood flow, and stomach tension and causes deeper, slower patterns of respiration. With a few simple additional exercises, this technique can also bring about a mood of calm, relaxed anticipation for the task ahead.

All the relaxation techniques we discuss here work well to counter blocking once it sets in, *but* they work best if employed *preventively*. Use them before you sit down to write and any time during the process that you feel physically stiff or mentally distracted. Most can be used immediately; some take practice before they can be applied with precision. In general, the more diligently you practice them, the better they work.

Physical Exercise

Anyone who exercises regularly knows the benefit of pumping fresh oxygen into weary brain cells. Getting out and jogging a few miles, playing a few sets of tennis, or swimming a few laps can be an extraordinarily refreshing thing to do, especially at the end of a long, tough day of slaving over a cold typewriter.

When you feel your energy and inspiration ebbing, push yourself back from your desk and do a few push-ups or sit-ups. Virtually any exercise at all will do—yoga asanas, isometrics, ballet positions, whatever you're comfortable with will counteract the build-up of muscle tension that any writer experiences. If you're working at home, take a break and go out for a brisk walk. Slip on your jogging shoes and put in a few miles at the track. (The bibliography includes various exercise books that may be of interest to you.)

Progressive Muscle Relaxation

Progressive Muscle Relaxation (PMR) is a highly systematic procedure for mechanically relaxing specific muscle groups, one by one in an orderly progression throughout the body, by tightening them up, holding them as tense as possible for a moment or two, then relaxing them far below the level of initial tension. First developed by a Chicago physician, Edmund Jacobson, in the 1920s, PMR and its numerous derivatives have been used in the treatment of a wide variety of physical and emotional disorders.

The PMR process usually starts with the extremities, the hands or feet, and moves up through the arms or legs, pelvis, stomach, chest, shoulders and neck to the scalp and the muscles of the face. The number of major muscle groups involved varies, but usually includes about a dozen. Here's an extract from one PMR routine:

> Begin with your right hand and arm. With your right hand resting on the arm of the chair, make a tight fist and hold it. Tense the muscles of this hand and forearm as tightly as you can. Hold them. Notice how the muscles pull across the top of the hand, in the fingers, and in the upper and lower part of the forearm.
>
> Now relax, let this arm and hand drop and go completely limp. Pay close attention to the feeling of relaxation in these muscles. Notice how their tension gives way to greater relaxation than before. Focus all your attention on helping the relaxation become as complete as possible.
>
> Now once again, with this same hand, make a tight fist and hold it. Again notice how the muscles tense and pull in your arm and forearm. Now relax it. Feel how the relaxation flows throughout the hand and arm. Your hand and arm will become more and more relaxed, more deeply relaxed than ever before.

The procedure then moves on to focus on the right biceps muscle, the left hand and forearm, the left biceps muscle, the shoulders, the eyes, eyelids, face, jaws, forehead, scalp, neck, chest, stomach, thighs, calves, and feet. In each case, the target muscle group is selected, tensed, relaxed, tensed once more, then relaxed again deeply for the last time. Each muscle group becomes distinctly more relaxed after the exercise than before.

You should practice PMR in a reclining chair or a couch, so you can completely relax all your muscles yet remain supported by the chair rather than having to maintain slight levels of tension just to keep your posture. Because practicing PMR will sharpen your ability to discriminate between tense and relaxed muscles, you can learn to concentrate only on those that are excessively strained. When you are able to differentiate in this way, you have gained enough muscle control so that you can apply relaxation during your daily work routines. (A more extensive discussion of PMR can be found in Tasto and Skjei's *Spare the Couch*, listed in the bibliography.)

Blocked writers find that PMR is particularly appropriate for relaxing the neck, eyes, and hands. To relax your eyes, follow these steps: First squeeze them tightly shut, then open them wide. Next move them from side to side, slowly, making them track as far as possible in each direction. Do this ten times for each eye. Then move them up and down, again tracking as far as you can without straining. Do this also ten times for each eye. Finally, rotate them along the outside perimeter of the eye socket. Do this clockwise five times, then reverse the direction and do the same thing counterclockwise five times.

You can add to the benefits of PMR by controlling your breath. Simply breathe deeply, from the abdomen rather than the chest. Breathe slowly, counting to ten as you inhale, then to ten again as you exhale. Do this six times, following the passage of air down into your lungs and out again. Blocked writers invariably report feeling the calming effect of this simple exercise immediately.

Follow the eye exercise with head rotation. Drop your

head forward onto your chest. Slowly swing it to the right, making a complete circle. Then do the same thing in the opposite direction. Allow the full weight of your head to pull against your neck and shoulders. Keep the motion continuous and even. You will feel the tension lifting from the muscles of your upper back and neck.

The Relaxation Response

A number of physiology researchers, notably Dr. Herbert Benson of Harvard's Thorndike Memorial Hospital, believe there is a natural counter-response to the fight-or-flight reaction, one that produces thorough physical relaxation and which can be deliberately evoked by following a simple five-step procedure. Benson calls this stress antidote the Relaxation Response. He has conducted extensive, carefully controlled research studies to test its validity and the best ways to elicit it. Among the benefits Benson feels result from practicing the Relaxation Response are reduced levels of blood lactates (associated with decreased anxiety) and increased alpha brainwaves, thought to be related to a heightened sense of calm and well-being.

Benson has distilled the essential components of a variety of Western and Eastern consciousness disciplines that he believes have the ability to call forth the Relaxation Response. He argues that producing this state requires no special training and can be done by following these simple steps:

1. Sit comfortably in a quiet environment.

2. Close your eyes.

3. Relax your muscles. (The PMR method works well here to complement the Relaxation Response.)

4. Focus your attention on your breath, following it as it goes in and out.

5. Maintain a passive but alert mental attitude, one of detachment from your thoughts—this is often accomplished by simply repeating a simple sound or word (e.g., *one*) to yourself.

These steps can be done at your desk—before, during, or after writing—any time you feel tense and need to relax. Benson suggests practicing the technique twice daily for ten to twenty minutes each time.

Traditional Meditation Techniques

Having learned Benson's technique, many writers have gone on to become interested in more traditional meditation practices, such as those taught by the Transcendental Meditation organization or any one of many other Eastern and Western spiritual disciplines. Some state that they receive even greater benefits from the more intense practice and community setting these disciplines provide than they gained from the Relaxation Response.

Accurate and comprehensive discussion of the differences among various meditative traditions surpasses the scope of this book, but an overview of the topic can be found in *Self-Psyching* by Michael Werthman, listed in the bibliography. One caution: Not all meditative practices are designed to *calm* the body and mind. Some have quite the opposite effect, of intensifying rather than lulling or tranquilizing your consciousness. Be sure you understand the objective of any meditative training you try out.

Intentional Imagery

Relaxation of the body is essential, but you also need to work on deliberately relaxing your mind when blocking makes you tense and anxious. Mental relaxation will happen naturally to some extent as an inevitable concomitant of physical relaxation, but blocked writers usually need an additional technique, such as visualization. Because the imagination tends to work more fluidly and powerfully when you're already physically relaxed, it's best to use the imagery procedure as a postscript, after you practice PMR, the Relaxation Response, or Traditional Meditation Techniques.

Relaxing with a pleasant mental scene, a fantasy, used to divert your attention away from a less pleasant reality, is something we do all the time. We usually call it daydreaming. Intentional Imagery practice differs from daydreaming only in that it is deliberate, is actively guided by the blocked writer himself, and is focused on the same or similar scenes each time.

The scene is usually drawn from a particularly strong memory, one that stands for peace and tranquility. Typical scenes described by our students and writing acquaintances have included: a canoe trip on a calm lake, a lush mountain meadow, a sleeping cat, a flower, a candle flame, a hot beach, a sail on a quiet bay, and a snowy winter scene. *Any* image that symbolizes relaxation to you will work. Sometimes working through a physical relaxation practice causes your mind to turn to such a scene or memory spontaneously. When it does, note the scene and use it again in the future.

Here's the way imagery works: Sit in a relaxed position. Shut your office door. Close your eyes gently and let the image slowly appear in your mind. Let it completely absorb and preoccupy you, to the point, if possible, of re-experiencing its sensations, colors, sounds, and emotions vividly. Don't force it; just let your absorption take place naturally, let the scene emerge in your mind. Continue to concentrate on maintaining your state of deep muscle relaxation while you practice the imagery technique.

Imagery practice clears your mind of the obsessive distractions that plague you when you're tense and worried. Instead of ruminating to the point of mental exhaustion, or skipping nervously from one trivial preoccupation to another, the experience of an intense, prolonged, but pleasant and relaxing image prepares you for thorough concentration on your writing task. It may take some practice to make this technique work well, but if done correctly it will make you more alert and more receptive to the detailed textures and contours of the topic at hand.

Pursue Other Interests

Some blocking stems from sheer mental exhaustion: print overdose . . . terminal literacy. Relentless exposure to nothing but those infernal little black marks marching across the page. This kind of blocking isn't as bad as not being able to get started at all, but it can be quite painful and frustrating in its own right.

"So one lights a fresh cigar; or chats with one's wife; or takes down a volume of poetry (Yeats for me) as a change of pace; or strolls around the block. Such interludes very often give the unconscious time to do the work for you."

— ARTHUR SCHLESINGER

Our prescription here is simple. Switch to some other kind of activity, one that engages different parts of your mind and body, for a while. Go out for a bite to eat. Make a phone call. Chat with a co-worker. If you can, take up a more physical activity. Go for a walk. Run up and down the stairs. If you're working at home, go out and pull weeds for an hour.

Adjust the carburetor. Sweep the floor. Admire your stamp album. Listen to an old Cole Porter tune. Take up needlepoint. Have a tepid (not hot) shower and a glass of wine (a little alcohol is a fine way to help you relax, but keep it under control). Anything that has the potential to offer you an engrossing break from your frustration as you sit there, stuck in the web of words, will help refresh you, at any stage of the process, whenever you feel your energy waning.

"Having drunk a pint of beer at luncheon—beer is a sedative to the brain, and my afternoons are the least intellectual portion of my life—I would go out for a walk of two or three hours."

— A.E. HOUSMAN

A RELATIVE, TO WILLIAM FAULKNER: *"Bill, are you drunk when you write those stories?"*
FAULKNER: *"Not always."*

GETTING TO KNOW THE INTERNAL CRITIC

The prewriting stage is your opportunity to come to terms with your nemesis, the internal critic. Unless you devote some time here at the start of the process to learning to recognize his voice so that you can keep it from obstructing your work, you'll have to contend with him later, and your resentment about the struggle will make it hard for you to use his perspective effectively in the revision stage, when his comments are not only useful but necessary.

You first need to simply get a better idea of who your critic is, when he tends to jump up and lay a suppressive hand on your shoulder, and what he likes to say when he evaluates your thoughts, your plans, your concepts, and your point of view. At this stage of the process, he doesn't yet have an actual draft or the beginnings of one to criticize, but you'll find he's just as intrusive as if he did. As random thoughts and possible phrasings drift through your mind, that annoying little voice you hear telling you why they're not quite good enough is his, and you must become intimately familiar with it if you want to tame him.

In our work with blocked writers, we've found two techniques that work well, individually or combined, to clarify an internal critic to his or her host: Portray the Critic and Dialogue with the Critic.

Portray the Critic

This is another useful application of imagery. Instead of relaxing you, however, it's intended here to give you a better picture of your critic and thus a familiarity that will allow a little constructive contempt for him.

The image you are to create is that of the critic as a person: how he (or she, or they) looks, behaves, sounds, and how he seems to be feeling. You may find the image is that of a real person from your past. Or it may be a composite of different people, a whole chorus of critics. Then again, what sometimes comes to mind is the image—a very vivid and distinct one for many blocked writers—of a person the writer has never seen before.

Eric's image of his own internal critic is that of a large, balding, heavy-jawed bulldog of a man, casting a manic glare at everything around him. His teeth are clenched, his brow furrowed. Waving a pipe and wearing a light blue suit and a dark, patterned tie, he paces rapidly back and forth, expounding in a dogmatic, belligerent manner on everything that seems vague or ill-conceived to him about Eric's current project. When forced to sit down and shut up, he can barely contain himself, and waits, puffing his pipe furiously, on the sidelines, blood in his eye, just waiting for a chance to jump in and point out something in the thoughts or words that isn't quite perfect.

In fact, the process of writing this book really drove him up the wall, since he was the object of attention much of the time and he felt, of course, that it was a terrible mistake to recommend that he be taken a lot less seriously. He was quite put out about that . . . sulked for days . . . but couldn't resist when asked to help with the revision of the draft. Then he really had fun. (And did a valuable job too.)

As you see, the description can be done with words. It can also be done with illustrations. These do not have to be polished, professional drawings. In fact it's better to make them deliberately crude and simple so you don't play into the critic's hands by worrying about how good they look.

Once you've sketched the critic, add yourself to the picture. When we've used this technique in the past, we've seen an extremely revealing relationship between the writer and the critic emerge on the page. For instance, a common image of the critic is a large, dominant, ugly figure in the center of the drawing. A much smaller, meeker, helpless-looking figure stuck off in a corner represents the blocked writer.

Often an unexpected result of the portrayal exercise is the introduction of a note of humor into the blocking dilemma. Blocked writers soon find it ridiculous to let themselves be so cowed by their own projections, by voices from the past that are, after all, only one of many aspects of their personality. Once they recognize this, their fears rapidly diminish, usually in direct proportion to the amount of playfulness that can be generated about this petty tyrant who delights in throwing his weight around.

Dialogue with the Critic

Now that you have a picture of your internal critic clearly in mind, you can move in a little closer and begin to get to know him a little better, to establish a workable relationship with him.

Start by closing your eyes and sitting silently for a minute or two. Think about your writing. What is it you have to do? What thoughts have you had about the best way to approach it? Let your mind pursue these issues for a while, then try to simultaneously focus on the doubts and fears that will also be starting to crowd into your mind, especially the doubts. These are the early warning signals of the internal critic at work, already beginning to erode your confidence and creative impulses.

If you can't quite hear his voice, provoke it into speaking up by saying something to yourself like, "O.K., here's my project and here's how I'm thinking of handling it. Now tell me what's wrong with it."

Remember Susan N., the blocked math teacher we described in Chapter 1? Here's how one of her dialogues with her internal critic went:

> SUSAN: Critic, I sense that you are against my project. Why are you making it so hard for me?
>
> CRITIC: What makes you think anything you have to say in writing will impress the bureaucrats downtown?
>
> SUSAN: My class had practically no discipline problems and the kids really learned. Their test scores were considerably higher than those of students in control groups. Most important, to me anyway, their motivation skyrocketed. I had kids volunteering for extra projects and completing them successfully. We used peer groups so that students who caught on quickly could help the slower ones. I had extra time for individual tutoring too.
>
> CRITIC: The way you describe it doesn't sound very professional. What theory did you test? What was your methodology? Do you have a model other teachers can follow or just a lot of impressions? I hope you're not going to hit me with a lot of vague statements that have no firm academic basis.
>
> SUSAN: I don't want to get bogged down in jargon right now. I know what my goals were and I know

that I had several strategies for attaining them. I got results and I have the data to back them up. I'll write this up the way I've explained it to parents and co-workers during conferences. I had no trouble communicating to them without resorting to bureaucratese.

CRITIC: Go ahead. Good luck. Telling it straight and simple will certainly be a novelty, if nothing else.

SUSAN: Relax. You're just worried that I might blow it, and it's making you sarcastic. I know what I have to say is important, and I know it can be said without sounding stuffy or pretentious.

Using this dialogue to expose her fears about the writing task, Susan is able to cope with her critic's harsh, slightly caustic voice in an effective way. She hears the objections he articulates, recognizing them as projections of her own fears, and rebuts them calmly and convincingly. At the end of the dialogue, her initial intention and her determination to carry it out are stronger than ever. Were she less aware of the critic's presence and function, all she could experience would be a strong, pervasive sense of discomfort and anxiety about the lack of academic rigor in her report, and the job would be much more difficult for her to accomplish.

Getting to know the internal critic is at the heart of learning how to unblock. We will refer to these techniques frequently in the following pages, especially in the case histories we describe in Part 3.

KEEPING A WRITER'S LOG

This may be the single most effective unblocking technique we know of. It has a wide range of applications, many of which we will discuss later in connection with other stages of the writing process. At the prewriting stage, the writer's log is most helpful as a way of exploring your general feelings about writing, blocking, and the internal critic. Dialoguing with your critic or portraying him, for example, is an excellent way to get a logging session started. Once you've drawn him out and exhausted his negative comments for the time being, you can move on to other, more general thoughts and feelings about yourself, the nature of the writing process, blocking, and your task.

The object of the logging technique is to help you demystify your own blocking. One simple reason blocking is so bewildering and frustrating for most writers is because, although they know that they themselves are causing it—no one else is preventing them from writing—they don't really understand what is going on inside them. They know it's confusing, they know it's paralyzing, but they're not clear about the specific sensations, thoughts, and feelings that being blocked seems to involve. They need to explore them further.

Start your log by getting your internal muttering down on paper (or tape) where it can be examined and analyzed and can start to teach you something about yourself. The log is a record of everything you can observe and capture about your apprehensions when you anticipate having to write or while you're involved in the writing process itself. (In Chapter 5 we discuss how to use a related technique, Nonstops, to help you unblock during the draft-writing stage. Here we just want you to become more familiar with your fears, your resistance to writing, especially those that show up as interference from the internal critic.)

The basic logging technique is free association. The only rule is: Write whatever comes to mind. Don't censor your thoughts. Let them wander freely and just try to follow along, recording their hops, skips, and jumps with pen or tape. Write about your feelings. Write about your thoughts. Write about the writing environment around you and your responses to it. (Record the date and time of day when you begin each new entry, so that you can later go back over the evolution of the experiences, thoughts, and feelings captured in the log.)

---

*"I write poetry. I use it as a form of mental relaxation.
I just let my mind go, and write, just describe
something without restriction or form, for myself."*

— AL MARTINEZ

Describe how you procrastinate, your mood and any changes in it, and the types of distractions and interruptions that you're susceptible to. What disrupts your concentration? What depresses you? What excites and inspires you? What relaxes you? What gets you going? What makes you feel that you've really accomplished something that day?

Include as much as possible; even the trivia that floats up to the surface of your mind holds clues to the emotions and ideas that are contributing to the block.

If you have trouble getting started, use a leading phrase like one of these to trigger a chain of associations:

When I try to write I feel (describe physical sensations as well as emotions) . . .
Writing reminds me of . . .
If I were perfectly confident, I would be able to . . .

When it goes well, the writer's log can help you get at the roots of block-related conflicts by illuminating writing and your attitudes toward it in ways that aren't otherwise accessible to you without recording them and then going back over them to see what they can teach you.

The longer you keep at it, the more you will begin to see certain repetitive patterns and themes emerge in the log. You'll notice yourself commenting over and over again on what you like, what you don't like, what distracts you, what inspires you, what makes you feel strong, what makes you feel weak, what blocks you, and what helps unblock you.

Here's an example entry from a log kept by Bill T., the blocked salesman we introduced in Part 1:

MY WRITING PROBLEMS:

I can't get the first words on paper without agonizing over them.

I can't strike the right balance between businesslike writing and the personal touch that makes letters more effective. My writing is either too stilted or too breezy, sometimes both.

I hate the way I feel when I have to write: trapped at a desk with nothing but a typewriter and a blank page before me.

BAD HABITS:

I go off and chat with people in the office when I should be writing.

I leave a few sketchy notes with my assistant and tell her to put the letter together, but I don't give her enough to work with.

I stare at the page and daydream, wishing I were somewhere, anywhere else.

THINGS THAT HELP ME WORK:

I do best when I tackle the writing soon after a meeting with the customer. There's a strong carryover from our conversation into what I put down on paper.

I'd like to talk it out with someone first, but I feel silly asking for help with something as routine as a letter.

I think best when I'm moving around, even pacing. Sitting in one place too long makes me feel like going to sleep.

Most of our students and writing friends find that at the prewriting stage the log doesn't demand a lot of their time.

Serious log-keepers write in their logs every day, for as little as ten minutes or as long as forty-five minutes to an hour, regardless of the type and length of writing tasks they happen to be engaged in. Like exercise and relaxation training, logging is a basic preventive habit, one that should be maintained constantly.

"I keep a daily journal. I have since 1959. Every day ever since. I buy a ledger, a book-size *ledger. (I've found that you get discouraged if the pages are too large because you have to write too much.) One page for each day. I find that filling that page, which I usually do an hour or so before going to bed (now it's such a habit I just can't think of doing without it) gets a lot of things out of your head. Also, you get used to putting words on paper."*

— IRVING WALLACE

A FRIENDLY EAR

One reason writing is so intimidating for a lot of people is because it's lonely: There's just you and the page—there's no one else—and, as we said in Chapter 1, virtually no external feedback. To combat the loneliness that can intensify anxiety about writing, seek company.

Like writing about your block in a log, talking it over with a friend can help you master it. You may be struggling with a topic that no one else can help you write about, but the powerful conflicts the block produces can be shared. Enlisting a sympathetic ear and a shoulder to lean on will help you relax and restore your sense of perspective. A good friend can reassure you that even though you may be blocking, you're not a failure, you won't always be blocked, and that writing is difficult for everyone at some point.

*"It helps if you have someone to talk to, it really helps.
I have my husband to talk to. It helps very much if I
say to him, 'I think I've painted myself into a corner.
Now I have three or four different solutions.' . . . we
discuss the solutions, and I pick the one I like best. I
don't think you can write a book completely alone."*

— JUDY KRANTZ

None of this will be new to you, but hearing it from a
believable source will make it more real. Not only will taking
a break to talk over your feelings with a friend help you
recover your self-esteem, it will also lend a little distance and
objectivity to your work. You will come back to it with
increased self-confidence and a willingness to review it dispassionately and constructively.

WRITE A PURPOSE STATEMENT

When you've gained a sense of equanimity about just getting
yourself to sit down to work, and you've made yourself
become more relaxed and attentive to the task at hand, your
next step is to define, in writing, as precisely and succinctly
as possible just what you're there to accomplish. You may
think you already know what you want to say, or the objective your writing is intended to accomplish, but trust us, it
will help no end in the unblocking process for you to take a
few minutes now to set forth a simple, clear summary of
what you want to say and why you need to say it. (Students
will recognize this as a "thesis statement," which tells a
reader what your subject is, what your position on the
subject is, and why that position seems right to you.)

Are you trying to put a second widget in every American household? Express your heartfelt appreciation for the
plastic samovar that Aunt Elinore sent you for Christmas?

Describe the operation of your firm's new computer in such simple language that it could be run by an adolescent spider monkey? Write it down.

It will also help you to keep in mind that most nonfiction, task-oriented writing serves the purpose of answering a question: Why should someone buy this product? What did our research study conclude? What is the history of the American prison system? Why should someone attend this fund-raiser? Formulating your central question will help you state your purpose. And then, having determined the ultimate destination of the job, you will begin to see which materials and organizational patterns will help you get there and which will probably just distract you into irrelevant byways. Your thinking and writing will become sharper and clearer because they become focused on a goal. By beginning to actively limit and subordinate your choices, you will begin to decrease your anxiety about writing. The task will begin to seem less intimidating.

The purpose statement is not only a destination, it is also a touchstone, a beacon that you can always look to in order to get your bearings. In the following pages, we will repeatedly suggest that you refer back to it as you work through the writing process in order to check your progress and realign your direction, if necessary.

THE INFORMATION MAGNET

You're a volunteer, working on the staff of a historical preservation society that wants to catalog and protect all the old architectural masterpieces in your city. The president of the society has just called you into her office and begged you to help them prepare a short newsletter article on the historical buildings in your neighborhood. Moved by the intensity and fervor of her idea, you agree, but as soon as you leave the office your heart jumps up into your throat: What do *you* know about architectural history? Where do you go to find out about it? Besides, you haven't written since high school and, as you now recall all too vividly, you weren't that good at it back then. Your mind goes completely blank.

This is a recurrent problem for blocked writers. They're given a task, an idea, a topic, but left entirely on their own when it comes to fleshing it out, to digging up the references and background material that many of their assignments require.

But handling the problem is simple. It just takes application and perseverance, plus a basic familiarity with the information-gathering techniques that any writer uses to research a topic.

Research Reading and Taking Notes

The first thing to do is to find out what other people have said about your subject and how they've gone about presenting it in writing. Even though the topic may seem entirely new and even exotic to you, rest assured that somewhere, at some time, someone has already written about it.

"Insufficient knowledge is an incentive to me. I then take a great deal of pleasure from learning. I have a very well-rounded reference library, so I hardly ever have to go to the university or public library for materials in the course of my writing because I have so much encyclopedic help. The only trouble with that is that it can be so absorbing, so interesting, that I get distracted."

— NORMAN CORWIN

The logical place to start your search is the local public or college library. Just getting to know more about the general field that you're working in can lead you into fresh avenues of creativity. And don't stop researching when you start to write. Keep learning all you can, even as you move on into draft writing and revising. You'll find that it constantly adds stimulation to your work, and helps relieve your anxiety by making you feel more and more knowledgeable about your subject matter.

Not only can reading critically provide you with useful information, it can also show you in detail how other writers have organized their thinking about the subject, what kind of slant or perspective they took on it, and what kind of audience they were appealing to. These kinds of precedents can be invaluable guides for your own work. In other words, read not only to find out *what* other writers can tell you, but also *how* they went about coping with the same issues and basic facts you're dealing with, how they constructed their own strategies for helping a reader follow and understand their line of thought. If you have access to model texts in your area, so much the better. (We know, for instance, of more than one research institute, entirely dependent on winning competitive grants and contracts to keep its doors open, that keeps files of all successful past proposals. We've recommended to one of these that it also keep files on past proposals that *didn't* work, so that negative as well as positive models can be consulted.)

"I make a lot of notes. There's something less frightening about rough notes. Notes are a useful device because you're under no tension when you write them."

— IRVING WALLACE

Take notes as you read. It's an important part of the process. Because writing engages the motor neurons that govern hand-eye coordination, it brings other areas of the brain more actively into the critical-thinking process that this kind of reading requires. The notes you take while reading another writer's work will lay the foundation for your own, as words, phrases, concepts, organizational possibilities begin to stir your own creative juices. And, furthermore, you'll find that you're getting words on paper without anxiety, an experience that helps you get ready for draft writing.

But working with books in the library is just the beginning. What you need to do is turn into an information magnet. As you become more involved with the subject and more knowledgeable about it, you'll find that you also become more sensitized to anything in the world around you—anecdotes, newspaper stories, statistics, allusions, references—that may pertain to your work. Flashes of insight will begin to hit you at the oddest times, in the damndest places—while talking to a friend at lunch, while waiting at a corner for a light to change, or while gazing blankly at cars around you as you ride home at night after work.

You need a system for plucking up and recording scraps of fact and fancy as they float to the surface of your mind or appear in the world around you. The classic tool for note-taking is the humble 3 x 5 index card. More potboilers, tearjerkers, and blockbusters (as well as serious dramas, documentaries, and dissertations) have first seen light as scribbled notes on a batch of 3 x 5 cards than you can shake an old rubber band at.

"I keep pads and pens all over the house, in any place that I'm likely to be . . . a stationery store cuts up huge blocks of yellow paper just the size I want. They drill a hole in it, and I stick a pen in the hole, so there's always a pen available . . . I always have a pad and pen in my purse, too."

— JUDY KRANTZ

Using the cards is entirely straightforward. Carry some with you everywhere. Whenever a pertinent thought, phrase, or reference occurs to you, jot it down. One entry per card. Then just let them accumulate, preferably in a file box. In our discussion of the next stage in the writing process, we describe a range of ways to organize this raw material into a coherent whole.

Talk to An Expert

Cardinal Rule No. 293 of the writing business: No matter what you're working on, you can always find someone around who knows more about it than you do. Take advantage of this fact. If you're working on an architectural preservation survey, for example, you would want to talk to the city's planning department, to local architects, and to the people in such federal agencies as the National Endowment for the Arts, all of whom would be able to shed some unique light on your subject. You would also consider talking to the people who have lived or worked in the historical buildings; they might be able to provide invaluable anecdotal material. And you would use one contact to lead you to another, by simply asking if they knew of someone else you should see.

Sitting down with an experienced, talkative source is the most direct and reliable way to gather information. It also has the bonus of making you more excited about your subject. An ordinary hour's conversation with an expert will unfailingly plant at least one seed for a new angle or approach. Go off and let it germinate and blossom, then, if you're feeling barren later, come back for a second round.

LISTS

Stacks of 3 x 5 cards have a natural way of becoming lists. As your data bank grows, distinct themes and patterns will begin to emerge. An idea will begin to expand, to fill out as you collect more information, to become central to your task. And using the 3 x 5 index cards will allow you the flexibility of shuffling and reshuffling to try out new arrangements of your material. When these tentative orderings get written down on a page in such a way that they can be perceived all at once, as a whole, you've moved one step closer to organizing—and one step closer to the knowledge that you can handle your subject securely.

Listing is the precursor of a ranking and ordering process that leads logically to outlining, which we discuss in the next section. Basically, of course, lists are a mnemonic device; they keep you from forgetting something. And in a detailed and highly complex process like writing, this function is important. It helps you remember inspired thoughts and constantly reassures you that you have a solid collection of information and ideas to work from.

For all their apparent simplicity—or perhaps *because* of it—lists serve a wide variety of important functions in the writing process, and we refer to them more than once in

---

"List-making is one of the simplest, most direct methods of increasing one's conceptual ability. People often compile lists as memory *aids (shopping lists, 'do' lists). However, lists are less frequently used as* thinking *aids. List-making is surprisingly powerful, as it utilizes the compulsive side of most of us in a way which makes us into extremely productive conceptualizers."*

— JAMES ADAMS

---

the following pages. They can, for example, be used as a consolidation and focusing tool, to collect as many divergent thoughts and angles as possible on a given topic. They can sum up the major questions that the writing must answer for your readers. And they can act as a compositional police force, making sure that you don't forget any of the countless routine procedural matters that nearly every piece of writing entails.

Let's take a look at a couple of these functions more closely. Listing the questions that your writing must answer is an excellent way to gain a fresh perspective on material that may have become stale from overexposure. It's a good way to check on how well reader expectations and information are being interrelated in your work.

Suppose, for example, you're a chemist and you're writing a progress report on a new industrial cleanser. Here are some of the basic questions you might want to keep in mind when you write and when you go back to see how well what you've written is going to communicate to your readers.

- What problem have we attempted to solve?

- What procedures have we followed to obtain our results?

- What problems have we encountered that caused us to revise our initial assumptions about this product?

- How much more time would we need to obtain definitive results?

- How will our research affect other areas within the company—design, production, and marketing, for example?

- What's our next step?

Once you've compiled a *thorough* list of such broad questions, rank them according to your reader's need to know. If your audience includes several readers whose priorities differ, you may want to consider breaking the report down into sections addressed to specific reader interests (as we do in Part 3 of this book), or use headings that will attract the attention of some readers but allow others to bypass information that isn't relevant to their concerns.

A second very common type of list is the catchall, or flypaper, list. These serve one simple function: to generate and capture an abundance of different thoughts on your topic. They work like this: Start by writing your subject at the top of a sheet of paper. Then, without looking at your notes, give yourself three minutes to simply list everything that comes into your head or that you remember from your information-gathering stages that's connected with the topic. Include it all, no matter how far-fetched or trivial it may seem at the moment. When your time is up, reread the list once or twice, then set it aside to incubate. After a few minutes (or hours, if you're not working under a tight deadline) come back to it and amend it so as to correspond to the insights that this brief recess has allowed you.

BRAINSTORMING

Sometimes six heads are better than one in coming up with new angles and slants on a topic, especially when that one is beginning to feel as though its brain cells are afire. If you work in an environment where you can call on friends or colleagues to lend you their gray matter for an hour or so, try Brainstorming. Bring them together in a private place to discuss the writing project. Before you begin, make sure the ground rules are clear to all involved:

- Everyone is to be as imaginative as possible. The idea is to come up with whatever new and different concepts, perspectives, points of view will move you forward, no matter how wild or outrageous they may seem at first. The only taboo is criticism or contradiction of another person's suggestions. (The critic is not welcome here.) A contribution by one participant can be picked up and developed or adapted by another participant, but the basic spirit of the group is one of cooperation, not competition.

- There is no single "right" answer.

- Everyone is to try to express as many different possibilities as he or she can dream up. In brainstorming, quantity leads to quality.

- Cover familiar ground first, then move off into uncharted conceptual territory.

- Record the entire session—either by taping it or by having one member of the group take notes.

The idea is to promote enough synergistic group energy that *everyone* catches fire, loses his or her inhibitions about sounding dumb or looking foolish, and makes a contribution.

Some additional ways to make a brainstorming session as productive as possible:

- Use a round table, to pre-empt the development of a hierarchy based on seating position.

- Hold the session in a fresh setting, not in the same office or conference room where you usually have group meetings.

- Use blackboards or tack up large sheets of paper on the wall so that ideas can be displayed graphically to the entire group.

- Hold the meeting at a time of day when everyone is alert and fresh. Usually the mid-morning to mid-afternoon interval works best.

- One member of the group should explain the purpose and ground rules of the session and keep things moving, but everyone should understand that there is no one leader among the participants.

GETTING FIRED UP

O.K., so you've taken charge of your writing environment, you've relaxed, you've made peace with your internal critic, and you've begun to explore and understand your material. What's next?

Motivation. As well as informed, you also have to be excited about your topic in order to unblock and handle it well. You need to engage the heart as well as the brain to transform the process from being halting and rough to surer and smoother.

Reading for Inspiration

Reading the work of other writers can provide more than just factual information and conceptual or structural guidelines—it can also be tremendously motivating. Most professional, full-time writers are also voracious escape, entertainment, and inspirational readers. They read for stimulation as well as information. Even the daily paper offers enough opinion and color, especially on the editorial page, to capture your attention and draw you into the web of words. (Most straight news stories don't offer enough excitement— they tend to play it safe and bland in order to avoid offending any particular group of readers. Look for an article or editorial that treats an issue you have strong feelings about. Or look for the by-line of a writer whose opinions usually manage to excite or outrage you.)

"I have a passion for newspapers—I read all the New York dailies every day, and the Sunday editions, and several foreign magazines too. The ones I don't buy I read standing at news stands. I average about five books a week—the normal-length novel takes me about two hours. I enjoy thrillers and would like some day to write one."

— TRUMAN CAPOTE

---

*"Or I will knock off and read something that I think
will stimulate me . . . there is no fuel so rich, no octane
so high as Shakespeare, or the Bible."*

— NORMAN CORWIN

Eventually, as you read more and more for inspiration, you'll begin to develop favorites, certain pieces that become inspirational touchstones for you, classics that you return to again and again to renew your vision. For one of our writing friends, the essays of E. B. White serve this function. Every time he rereads *One Man's Meat* he finds himself rediscovering his fascination with the craft of writing. With each new reading, he finds something new and powerful to admire about White's supple personal style. And that, as he puts it, is just the kind of fascination he needs to help get him through the slumps in his own writing and provide fresh models for his Constructive Plagiarism exercises, which we discuss soon.

"Before I start writing a novel, I read Candide *over
again so that I may have in the back of my mind the
touch-stone of that lucidity, grace and wit."*

— W. SOMERSET MAUGHAM

The Treasury

Part of the pain of focusing intently on one subject, which is a mandatory part of successful writing, is that you begin to feel that other things of value—observations, insights, discoveries—are being neglected. Sometimes, as you're playing Information Magnet, serendipitous but irrelevant little nuggets of fact and fancy crop up along the way. The feeling that they're slipping through your fingers because you have a job to do, one that requires intense concentration of you, can make you resentful and irritated and can foster contempt for your task, which can in turn exacerbate your block.

You need a way to capture and preserve these passing gems, to keep from feeling that you're missing something when you write. Furthermore, saving them gives you a supply of germinal seeds for later jobs.

Like squirrels hoarding up acorns against winter scarcity, most people we know who do much writing learn to keep files of intriguing concepts, well-turned sayings, and crisply rendered arguments. Then, when they need a lead to get them going, when the words won't come, or they need a slightly different slant on a familiar topic, they just riffle through their collection. Even if they don't find precisely what they're looking for, evidence of abundance in the midst of an internal drought is some comfort in and of itself.

Eric keeps a treasury file devoted exclusively to absurdity: old copies of especially delightful stories from *Punch*, the English humor magazine, an occasional obtuse fortune cookie aphorism, and other quaint and quirky little jewels.

Develop your own writing treasury. It can be anything from a series of manila folders to a large shoebox placed in a convenient spot in your office, or wherever else you do your writing. Jot down the interesting ideas you run across (use those ubiquitous 3 x 5 index cards again), even if you don't at the moment see their relevance to the work you're involved with. Some of these notes will be your own invention, others the work of another inspired craftsman. If you hear something that you think is especially well said, write it down. Clip newspaper articles, cartoons, ads. Keep copies of well-written letters, memos, reports, and articles to serve as inspirational models for your own work.

"I have a file cabinet. In it is a file on each character. I research for months and months and months before I start. Then I take out the files that are germane to the chapter I'm working on. And I'll have all kinds of stuff in there. I'll have things I clipped from magazines. I'll have pictures of what I think they might look like. If I see a picture of a room that looks like a room that one of my characters might live in, I'll tear it out and put it in my file. I have all sorts of things I wrote down. And I'll read it over and from that will come some starting place. I think preparation is essential. I don't start empty-headed."

— JUDY KRANTZ

Epigraphs

One thing you'll almost surely find yourself collecting in your treasury is epigraphs. Epigraphs (literally, a "writing before") are borrowed quotations set at the beginning of a text to epitomize its theme and tone. (You probably noticed the Flaubert lament quoted at the beginning of this book.)

A short line or two that adroitly sums up the essence of what you're trying to convey in your writing can quicken your thoughts. It can suggest a theme, a style, or a tone you'd like to replicate. Also, as we explain in more detail later, a pithy sentence or two on your topic can ease you into the actual writing by triggering creative, new associations that you rapidly scrawl on the page. Because this writing is not your "real" theme, you may be able to produce it easily and quickly, and you may be so pleased with your facility that you can circumvent your block and prepare yourself to write the draft without undue anxiety.

Epigraphs don't have to be solemn. They can be playful. And you can use phrases other than quotations from well-known authors. You can make up your own. You can include advertising jingles, cartoon captions, limericks, even odd names that double as puns: "Couth, Ept, & Ruly, Attorneys-at-Law," or "Noah Vale, Biblical Patriarch."

The best sources for conventional epigraphs are *Bartlett's Familiar Quotations* and *The International Thesaurus of Quotations*, familiarly known as the *ITQ*. In Bartlett's work, first published in 1882, quotations are arranged by author, but the book is also indexed by topic and by keyword. However, if you want a suitable quotation on a specific subject rather than the *bon mots* of a particular author, the *ITQ* is a better place to look, since it is arranged by category of idea, starting with *Ability* and ending with *Zen*. (Its publishers describe it as a work designed for readers who "will very likely turn to it less often to recall a familiar saying than to find fresh words that eloquently express and enlarge ideas of their own.")

Constructive Plagiarism

When you just can't bear to face the effort involved in putting your own words on the page, it can help you to begin by putting someone else's down. It won't make your block any worse than it already is, and it will bring you into intimate contact with the texture and tone of another writer's

---

"I hasten to add here that imitation is natural and necessary to the beginning writer. In the preparatory years, a writer must select that field where he thinks his ideas will develop comfortably. If his nature in any way resembles the Hemingway philosophy, it is correct that he will imitate Hemingway. If Lawrence is his hero, a period of imitating Lawrence will follow."

— RAY BRADBURY

---

work. Done thoughtfully, imitative writing can loosen you up, begin to give you the feel of getting words on paper, amuse and inspire you, and give you an appetite for moving on to your own thoughts and phrases.

Select a passage that seems especially well written, elegant, succinct, or funny to you. Read it through with an ear for the special qualities of voice and tone that make the text characteristic of that particular author. Then take pen in hand and, playfully at first, try to cast a few lines of your own topic into the same style. Use much of the same diction and phrasing of the original, but try to infuse your content matter into this framework. Presto, you'll be writing . . . without qualms, psalms, or sweaty palms.

Here, for example, is how Hemingway might have written a follow-up report if he had been a salesman just returning from an unsuccessful call on a prospective client:

> I had gone to his office, to the noise and clatter and harshness when the room whirled and I needed to make it stop, hours on end, talking to him, feverish, when I knew that that was all there was, and the strange excitement of sitting down in the chair and not really knowing who it was there in the office with me, and the room all unreal in the neon glare and so boring that I had to begin again unknowing and not caring in the room, sure that this was all and all and all and not caring.

Hamming It Up

Imitative writing leads naturally to imitative roleplaying, in which you take on all the aspects and mannerisms of a model character, one who isn't blocked, so as to momentarily escape from your own sense of constraint. The experience of enlisting your imagination into *acting* confident about writing, we've found, has surprising carryover effects into the real writing process; it really does help allow blocked writers to *become* more confident.

Choose someone you know and respect as a role model. You might like to play Shakespeare, but you'll find that picking a teacher, friend, or colleague will give you more practical, down-to-earth material to work with, since you actually have some idea of what this person's attitudes and behavior are like.

Warm up for your role by reading something that your model has written, by speaking as she or he does, or even by acting out her or his movements and gestures. Become consciously dramatic and theatrical. No one is watching, so let yourself go.

Because roleplaying permits you to treat the writing produced by your newly assumed personna as something other than your "real" work, you're able to short-circuit the internal critic and become more creative, more flexible, and less judgmental. Roleplaying can completely invert your normal character. You find yourself becoming authoritative instead of ambivalent, earthy instead of refined and delicate, fluent instead of stiff. And once the performance is over, the critic can be called in to help you write a review. Here's an example:

A friend of Karin's, an engineer, was having enormous difficulty getting started on a report he had to write for his company. He had just been hired, and he didn't have a clear sense of how his boss and his co-workers regarded him. In other words, he didn't quite know his new role as a professional employee yet. Karin suggested that he try roleplaying, and that he assume the guise of a favorite teacher casually chatting with a group of students at lunch. How, she asked, would he go about communicating the contents of the report in that setting?

He sat quietly for a minute or so, feeling the role out, then began talking. His sentences were sharp, clear, and precise. He used examples well to explain the more technical points, and he referred effectively to his graphs and diagrams as he did so. Karin stopped him after a few minutes and told him to start right in drafting the report just as he'd been explaining it to her, as if he were still that same teacher addressing that same group of students in that same informal, direct, plain way.

4

Organizing Your Material

Y NOW, having worked through the prewriting stage, you possess the skills to take charge of your surroundings, dispel your excess tension, meet and master your internal critic, and start generating ideas, information, and excitement about your subject. As we said earlier, the problems you encountered at the first writing stage may recur again at other points in the process. You may, for example, find that you still get tense every time you sit down to write or even just think about writing, but you now know how to go about combatting that tension by making Systematic Relaxation a regular part of your writing routine.

On the other hand, even if you breezed through the prewriting stage, at this second stage of the process you may find that you've suddenly run into a psychological brick wall: You've got a stack of index cards or a page of notes, but you're suddenly feeling panicky, confused, and unsure about your next step. You urgently need to know how to go about transforming the information you've gathered, how to best relate this fact to that, to express the connection between this primary concept and that secondary one—in short, how to shape the material so that the reader gets the message.

In other words, you need *structure*, a scaffolding you can use while the edifice is going up. This can be a particularly intimidating problem on large, complex jobs, where the sheer bulk of the information you have to arrange and order can overwhelm you with alternatives for its most effective presentation. Yet this obstacle can arise as often on a short task—a one-page description of a product for a sales staff, a short business letter, and so on. Blocked writers drive themselves mad wondering what they should say first, what next, how they should end the piece. And the answers don't come easily.

But just as the block can occur at various stages of the writing process, so it can rear its inhibiting head according to the task you're trying to perform. Perhaps you had no trouble outlining your last memo, but finding the best organizational scheme for your new resumé is turning into a nightmare. That's the nature of blocking. It can happen to anyone, any time, at any point in the process. And it can happen to the same person at entirely different stages in the process on different jobs.

To help you cope with structure, we've included in this chapter a series of simple techniques for organizing your thinking and your text, showing you how to undercut the organizational blocking that you may encounter with any writing task.

Before you scan the techniques, let's review briefly what goes on during this organizational stage of the writing cycle. Essentially, this is the stage where you decide how you want your subject to enter the reader's mind, and therefore how you want to arrange your ideas on the page. Like drafting a blueprint, by showing yourself the contours of the whole job at the start of the process of composing it, you help set its boundaries and thus give yourself important reassurances that it is manageable, that it isn't more than you can handle in the time available. And by giving yourself an advance view of the whole job, by trying out different ways of ordering the material and presenting the subject to your audience, you also gain the security of knowing at each moment in the process just how far you've come already and how much you have left to do.

Another benefit of ordering the material in advance of writing is that you give yourself at least a tentative idea of where each piece of information you collect or create fits into the total framework. A frequent cause of blocking is the confusion that ensues when you try to hold the entire pattern in your head at one time. Persuading yourself to organize frees you up to focus on only one chunk of the job without losing your sense of its place in the work as a whole, or feeling that you're neglecting other aspects of the subject while you're working with only one.

The second stage of the writing process helps bridge the gap—an impassable chasm if you're blocked—between gathering information and ideas on index cards and actually sitting down to compose the first draft. The techniques described in this chapter fit into the middle of a natural progression that moves from making notes, to writing lists, to loose outlines, to increasingly more precise and hierarchical outlines, to free-association writing of rough draft sections, to entire drafts, and finally to a revised, polished, final text.

Unlike some of the other stages, where the blocking experience is one of painful empty-headedness, this second stage can confuse you with too many alternatives. A diabolical kaleidoscope shifts compulsively in your head, showing with each fractional turn a potential new pattern for your material. Your mind leaps inconclusively from one pattern to the next. You want to act impulsively, to reach out in irritation and bring the twirling patterns to a halt, to just throw it all together any-old-which-way, mumbling "What difference does it make anyway?"

Resist this impulse. Comfort yourself with the thought

that everything is still provisional at this stage. You're not yet locked into any particular format. The framework can always be changed later. (It does, naturally, get harder to restructure as you move along toward the final draft, but unlike other creative processes like sculpture or cooking, writing is limited only by time, not by any intrinsic constraints imposed by the medium itself. An essay cannot dry out and harden into a misshapen lump.) At this point in the writing process, all roads are still open to you.

But how do you decide which way to pile up the bricks of thought and word so that the structure is manageable and expressive? That's what we show you in this chapter. We begin by referring you back to your purpose statement and pointing you toward defining your audience. Knowing clearly what you're trying to accomplish and who your audience is will tell you where to begin your narrative. Profile a Reader and talk your ideas over with an objective Friendly Ear who can tell you whether you're clear and on target.

From that point on you're ready to use lists, outlines, and other simple organizational techniques that will give you the confidence to begin writing.

RETURN TO YOUR PURPOSE STATEMENT

In the previous chapter, we suggested that you state your purpose explicitly, in writing, so that you could relate your preparatory thinking to a specific discursive destination. If you're blocking at the organizational stage, go back to that purpose statement and review it again to get your bearings. Having collected a lot more information on your topic, you may find that your perspective on it and how to best deal with it has changed, and you may need to rewrite the statement to make it more exact.

There's an added benefit to this process. Not only do you clarify what you're doing, which always helps when you're feeling stuck, but you also slowly begin to appropriate the job for yourself. It may have come to you in the form of someone else's instructions, as a job assignment, but by analyzing it, redefining it, and restating it, you gradually make it your own. And by doing so, you become more involved in it, more interested in it, and more capable of accomplishing it.

THE FRIENDLY EAR REVISITED

You may want to revisit the Friendly Ear who helped you manage your feelings about your block and your self-esteem. A receptive colleague or friend can also help you unravel your organizational approach to your topic. Pick a sympathetic ear for this exercise, someone who is a good, intelligent listener, and someone who genuinely wants to take the time to listen to you carefully.

At first, just have him or her listen without responding, except to ask for minor clarifications. Lay out your thoughts about your material, your approach to it, your conceptual framework, and so on—but as simply as possible. Ask your listener to note anything especially good or especially confusing. (Often this part of the process alone will clear your head and give you new directions to pursue.)

Talk until you don't have anything else to say. Then, ask the Friendly Ear to feed the information back to you in simple language and to evaluate your organizational system. Now it's your turn to listen carefully. Does what you hear coming back to you differ from what you thought you just said? Is it coming back sounding better? Or worse? If it's worse, then you can identify the weak spots, places where your structure and thinking have to be made clearer or more complete. Some thoughts will need to be made more prominent in the narrative. Others will need to be toned down, so that they fade into the textual woodwork, or even vanish altogether.

In some ways, the role of the Friendly Ear at this stage

of the process parallels that of the Critical Reader, which we discuss next, but with an important difference. Precisely because your listener is a Friendly Ear, he or she can give you reasonable, objective feedback, but without the threatening critical overtones that a more impersonal respondent might convey. Working with the Friendly Ear first in this way introduces you to another person's perspective on your work, but also assuages your anxieties about receiving feedback, thus clearing the way for you to move on to more detached and potentially more rigorous reactions to your writing.

PROFILE A (CRITICAL) READER

Knowing who your audience is helps you to assign priorities to the information you wish to present: What should come first, be subordinated, and so on. For that purpose, it helps to Profile Your Reader—even if you must invent one. Try to make him or her slightly *critical* (maybe even mildly obtuse)

"I know there are a lot of writers who say to hell with 'the reader'; if he has to work to read me then let him work, if he wants to read me. I don't know what I feel myself. I guess I would fall somewhere in between the two extremes. I think the writer ought to help the reader as much as he can without damaging what he wants to say; and I don't think it ever hurts the writer to sort of stand back now and then and look at his stuff as if he were reading it instead of writing it."

— JAMES JONES

---

so as to alert you to the areas where your approach goes off on a tangent and poses the danger of boring your readers and losing their fickle attention. If there's one trait you can count on, it's the readers' impatience. They will want to know quickly why they should read what you've written. Their attention span is limited. They're very adept at scanning a page quickly to form an impression of whether or not there's anything they want to take a more careful look at. If they're attracted to what you've written and choose to reread it more thoroughly, they'll want you to carry them along through the text without their having to expend much energy following what you're saying. The more vividly and realistically you can portray this audience, the easier ordering your thoughts will be.

Having an idea (and an image) of Mr. or Ms. Critical Reader will help you understand when an idea hasn't yet been sufficiently developed, that you need another paragraph or two to explain it fully. Or you may discover that by bringing up a specific concept, you raise more questions than you answer; you'll have to reroute the narrative so as to bypass this danger zone or meet it head-on and expand your text to accommodate the reader's need for more elaboration.

You may also find that the opposite happens, that by creating a typical reader you realize that you don't need to explain certain aspects of the topic quite so extensively because the reader is already familiar with them.

Here's an example of an organizational problem having to do with how best to attract the reader's attention. A friend of ours, an ex-blockee, recounts the story of having to write a resumé for a job she was well qualified for and wanted badly. She had all the information she needed to write it—dates, names, addresses—and she was highly motivated to get it done and submitted before the deadline passed. But she was blocking. She couldn't make up her mind what to put first. Should she lead off with a straightforward, chronological list of her job experience (which wasn't all that impressive, since she'd just graduated from college a few years earlier), or should she try for a slightly more personal approach by writing up a brief statement of purpose or a succinct abstract of her occupational skills and goals?

And then there was the cover letter. She knew she could use it to fill in or reinforce the information in the resumé, but she wasn't sure what it should say. The more she thought about the possible alternatives, the more ambivalent and confused she got.

We suggested that she try working up a profile of the typical resumé reader. Since our friend knew the corporation she was applying to was large, hierarchical, and somewhat conservative, we suggested a few basic starting points that suited that milieu. Here's what she came up with:

> My typical reader in this company is someone in mid- or upper-level management, someone accustomed to making decisions about hiring and firing. It may be a woman, but I doubt it. I'm going to be realistic and figure that for the next decade or so, past discrimination about advancing women into management means that it will probably be a man.
>
> He's middle-aged, maybe in his early 50s. Three-piece suit, greying temples, air of distinction. Crisp. Experienced.
>
> This man knows what his needs are and he knows that he'll recognize a suitable candidate to fill them when he sees his or her qualifications and has a chance to conduct an interview. He's not afraid to make decisions, to select the half-dozen best out of the hundreds of resumés he's been getting, call them in for interviews, and scrap the rest. He trusts his judgment. And he does not have the time or the patience to wade through irrelevant information. But he's also flexible. He's looking for that special extra quality that makes one candidate stand out over another.
>
> So I know that my immediate objective is winning an interview with him. The overall goal is the job; but first I've got to make sure I'm not one one of those he

winnows out. So I should let him know that (a) I'm completely qualified for the position, (b) I've got something to offer that makes me uniquely suitable for it, and (c) I'm eager.

Having worked through this exercise, our friend's organizational blocking cleared up dramatically. She decided to be as businesslike as possible, to form the core of her resumé around her work experience, education, training, and references, listed in that order. She also decided to add a short summary of her career skills and goals at the top of the page, restricting it to no more than a line or two. Then she decided to use the cover letter to go into more detail about why she wanted this particular job and why she wanted to work for that particular company.

Her strategy worked. She got an interview . . . but didn't get the job. However, she did make a contact that led her to an even better opening in a second company where she's now successfully climbing the corporate ladder.

LISTS AGAIN

As well as the general mnemonic function that lists serve at every stage of the writing process, they have a specific application to blocking at the organizational stage. Let's say you've collected, in your previous incarnation as Information Magnet, an inch-thick stack of 3 x 5 cards. Now you want to figure out how to arrange them so that when you write up the draft, the steps the narrative moves through make sense to your reader.

You feel comfortable with your sense of purpose and your feeling for your reader, but you're having trouble figuring out how to order the information so that it follows the clearest, most expressive sequence possible. There seem to be so many possible arrangements. And the problem is compounded by the fact that you can't hold all the information in your head as you shuffle through the cards. What you need, in short, is a list. Instead of a stack of cards, you need a sheet or two of paper, on which all the information you've collected is consolidated and displayed for your review.

Once you've made the transfer from cards to list, you will automatically begin to engage that powerful ranking faculty everyone possesses: Certain entries will begin to stand out from the page as being of central importance. Others will naturally fall back into secondary positions, to cluster around the more important concepts that they support. So you will begin to shift items around, circling them and drawing long lines and arrows to show where they might be better positioned. Soon some shape will emerge from what was completely amorphous—and terrifying—before. Keep it up. You're on the verge of outlining.

OUTLINES

The chief benefit of any kind of outline when you're blocking at organizing your material is that it gives you a provisional

---

"Blocking is the panic of not knowing where to go next, and outlining is the way to avoid it . . . . I write from an outline. I don't sit down at the typewriter and expect words to come out. It starts as a general outline for the book, and then I break it down into chapter outlines, and each chapter I break down into scenes. I know where I'm going."

— JUDY KRANTZ

---

grasp of an overall pattern of interrelationships among different aspects of your subject—that is, it begins to show you a possible way to organize your material so as to make your point.

Most of us are familiar with the traditional outline form: Roman numerals for the major headings, followed by capital letters, Arabic numerals, lower case letters, and so on in descending order of significance. Though it has its uses, this type of outline also has a serious drawback: It forces you to impose a detailed hierarchy of relative values on the material from the start, by making decisions—often quite arbitrary—about which points are primary and which are ancillary. This pattern can force you into a rigid, inaccurate impression of your topic—so rigid that you feel paralyzed, unable to deviate from the format. We've all had the experience of working up an outline like this only to find that the more complete it became, the more strongly we suspected that the major heading for Part I was buried under subitem II.A.3. In other words, most of us have discovered that traditional outlining can be more trouble than it's worth.

There is a more flexible, intermediate type of outlining, one that doesn't commit you so quickly to so detailed a hierarchy, and thus allows you precious room for change and refocus when you're having trouble creating any kind of meaningful organizational system at all.

Spoke Outlines

The Spoke Outline is an ordering scheme that allows you to escape the problems of the more traditional outline model. It graphically reflects the incompleteness and absence of hierarchical order in your thinking at the early stages of the writing process, and it gives you room to easily expand, contract, or rearrange the elements of the outline. At the same time, it lends a preliminary form to your job.

You start the construction of a Spoke Outline by writing your Purpose Statement in the middle of the page. Use an oversize sheet if possible, to give yourself plenty of room. We've included an example of a Spoke Outline (see Figure 4-1) written by a student of Karin's in response to this

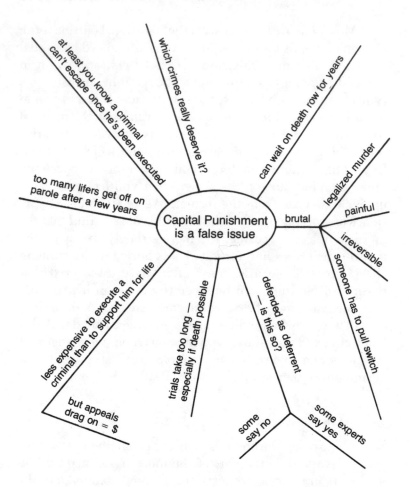

FIGURE 4–1 PRELIMINARY SPOKE OUTLINE

Some possible conclusions:
  — Cost, deterrence, and morality always discussed regarding
     capital punishment
  — Laws are inconsistent and confusing
  — System of justice is cumbersome and slow
*— We need to streamline system of justice and rewrite
     the laws to insure speedy and sure justice
*— Capital punishment is a red herring

assignment: "Demonstrate that capital punishment is a red herring."

The second step is to draw lines radiating out from the central statement, like the spokes of a wagon wheel. On these lines you write down all the key terms or ideas that you develop in response to the Purpose Statement. They're analogous to the major headings of a traditional outline, but because the spokes form a circle, you don't have to worry about ranking them at this stage of the organizing process. (Feel your tension subsiding?)

Add as many spokes as you think you'll need, then draw new lines branching out from each spoke—like third-level pieces angling out from the major braces. These are the places for examples, subordinate arguments, tangential concepts, logical links, and so on—all the related details that support key terms and major concepts. They correspond to the second- and third-level entries on a traditional outline, but the advantage of the Spoke Outline is that even these levels can be set down, developed, and rearranged without any need for decisions about ranking.

Some spokes will extend much farther than others and will require extensive subbranches. You will probably also find that some ideas or examples show up on several different branches. On the other hand, the appearance of a spoke without any subbranches may mean that you need to do more research on that idea, or that this spoke shouldn't be representing a major heading after all, but could be better placed under another one.

As your Spoke Outline grows, you will be able to see more and more clearly what your most important points are and how they relate to one another. Unifying themes and patterns will emerge. As with the traditional outline form, you may find that what you initially thought to be your central topic was only a tangential starting point. You can easily rearrange a Spoke Outline to reflect this evolution.

Figure 4—1 shows the initial thoughts and tentative conclusions of Karin's student; Figure 4—2 is his second Spoke Outline, derived from and constructed around one of the conclusions he drew from the first. Because it has a strong governing thesis under which all his secondary ideas can be logically arranged, the second outline is a blueprint for his essay. It was the key that unlocked his block.

Sentence Outlines

Once you've come up with a Spoke Outline that satisfies you and helps dissolve your block, you're in a good position to move on to the next step: collecting and arranging the separate entries from the Spoke Outline into the Sentence Outline, a sequence that more closely approximates the linear, hierarchical nature of an actual first draft.

You've already done most of the hard work—from here on it's just a matter of refinement. Remember that even the Sentence Outline is not rigid. You still have freedom to pursue other alternatives if they seem more appropriate to you. But now you *do* have a conceptual structure to work with, and that's what unblocking at the organizational stage is all about.

Here's how Karin's student transformed a Spoke Outline into a Sentence Outline. He used his second outline, which represented an evolution in his thinking from exploring the general topic of capital punishment as a false issue to focusing on this assertion: "Swift and sure justice is the real issue." Then he went back a step and simply listed all his second- and third-level ideas, terms, examples, and subordinate arguments. This page was only a list, not an outline; he made no attempt to arrange it in any particular order, but just started in at one spoke and moved methodically around the wheel, writing down everything he saw as he went along. The result looked like this:

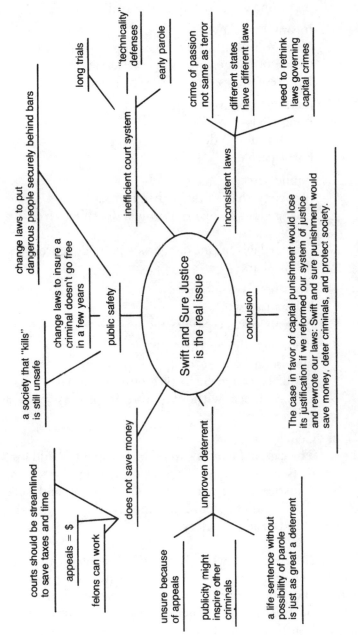

FIGURE 4–2 ADVANCED OUTLINE

Swift and sure justice is the real issue.

III. Inconsistent laws
Need to rethink laws governing capital crimes
Crime of passion not same as terrorism
Different states have different laws

II. Inefficient court system
Long trials
"Technicality" defenses
Early parole

I. Public safety
A society that "kills" is itself unsafe
Change laws to insure criminal doesn't go free in a few years
Change laws to put dangerous people securely behind bars

II. Does not save money
Felons can work
Appeals cost taxpayers money

II. Unproven deterrent
Uncertain because of appeal process
Publicity can even inspire other criminals
Life sentence without parole is just as great a deterrent

I. Conclusion
The case in favor of capital punishment would lose its justifications if we reformed our system of justice and rewrote our laws: Swift and sure punishment would save money, deter criminals, and protect society.

Then the student went back and designated the elements he thought could be worked into full sentences by assigning them numerals (shown at left margin above) and letters. The final result, which is virtually identical to a traditional outline, looked like this:

I. Introduction: The debate over capital punishment would be obsolete if we reformed our criminal justice system.

    A. Proponents and opponents agree that deterring criminals is essential.

    B. Both sides agree also that public safety must be safeguarded.

    C. While money is not the main issue, everyone wants to see tax dollars spent wisely and efficiently.

II. Argument

    A. No sentence can be an effective deterrent if criminals and others who contemplate crime believe they'll never be caught. Today the odds are all in their favor.

    B. Life sentences are reduced, executions are delayed, and both sentences are frequently overturned in our inconsistent, inefficient justice system.

    C. Today the taxpayer's money is squandered on lengthy appeals and costly trials regardless of the sentence.

III. Conclusions

    A. Make sure that criminals know the odds favor their being apprehended.

    B. Revise our laws to make them rational and to insure that once a sentence is imposed, it sticks.

    C. Reform court procedures to make them more efficient and therefore less costly.

Having arrived at this stage, our formerly blocked student had little further trouble with organization and was ready to begin fleshing out the outline as he moved on to the draft writing stage.

BULLETIN BOARDS, BLACKBOARDS, AND STORYBOARDS

When you're confronted with a job that involves a particularly complex organizational framework, or ongoing input from many contributors, you will find it helpful to be able to display the process in such a way that everyone involved has simultaneous access to proposed organizational arrangements as you work with them. The tool for accomplishing this display is nothing more complicated than the old-fashioned chalkboard or bulletin board (also known as a "storyboard" and used extensively in ad agencies and by many large engineering and aerospace firms in the preparation of team-written proposals). Even a large pad of paper, something to prop it up on, and a bunch of colored pens will do just fine.

Bulletin boards let you handle a lot of information all at once, and in a way that makes it graphically legible to a group. Having the work prominently displayed makes it possible for participants to keep track of one another's progress and thus to maintain continuity and consistency among different sections. Each writer or participant has the freedom to focus on a particular section of the entire job without losing his or her perspective on the whole work. And as the group's organizational thinking evolves, the workers can easily rearrange the placement and order of the data to redefine the entire outline or to rearrange subsections without upsetting the overall pattern.

To mount your ideas and topics on a bulletin board, we recommend using different colors to represent major headings, minor headings, examples, and so on, and a slightly larger index card, 4 x 6 inches. The 4 x 6 size gives you room to write large, but not so much room that you're tempted to put more than one entry on a card, or cram unrelated ideas together.

PREFABS

You may find that your material simply refuses to offer up its own organizational scheme, no matter how hard you try to push and poke it into shape. This happens to everyone, and it's immensely frustrating. You know that the most appropriate intrinsic structure is in there somewhere, but you seem to be getting farther and farther away from it, rather than triumphantly closing in on it.

Fear not. There is a completely reliable, last-ditch alternative—quite a respectable one, actually—to throwing in the towel or just continuing the futile struggle with your puddle of sand. Try using what one publisher friend of ours calls "desperation grids"—simple, prefabricated organizational schemes that are so broad they can be applied to virtually any topic. Most are traditional, time-honored strategies for arranging a text, even a very short one, and they work especially well when you're pressed for time and can't afford to work out all your alternatives. Occasionally harried or blocked writers find that the prefab makes a great foil: In the process of working to fit it to their subject matter, they inadvertently discover, by contrast, an intrinsic framework that will work much better.

Who, What, When, Where, Why

If your job includes a lot of factual material, such as a press release about an upcoming event, you may find that the five classic Ws of journalism work well as an organizational format. The categories are *who*, *what*, *when*, *where*, and *why*.

Simply list the five categories on one side of a sheet of paper and then slot in your information under the appropriate heading. Feel free to add, subtract, or alter the headings if you need to. For example, some press releases call for a category labeled "how" or "how much," and in many cases the "why" is self-evident or irrelevant.

The Five Ws Prefab is especially suitable for writing jobs in which you have to communicate a lot of circumstantial detail to readers who are so pressed for time that they won't bother to read past the first few lines if you don't start giving them what they want to know right away.

Beginning, Middle, End

Here is an organizational form borrowed from classical rhetoric: "Tell 'em what you're gonna say, say it, then tell 'em what you said." These three steps are a simplified version of classical rhetorical theory on how to structure a persuasive speech. The number of steps traditionally varied from four to seven or more. The basic skeleton included: introduction, statement of the theme or topic, a brief history or background discussion, presentation of the argument itself, rebuttal of anticipated objections and criticisms, and a summation in which the basic theme was again restated. This structure is especially well suited for speeches or other texts that may be delivered orally, as well as for writing jobs that have a particularly strong argumentative or persuasive dimension; but the form has been successfully applied to virtually every type of writing we know of (including poetry).

PEMS

PEMS is an acronym for "Physical, Emotional, Mental, and Spiritual." Where this organizational paradigm first arose is anyone's guess. Clearly it is so general as to be attributable to nearly every major school of thought, but its virtue is that it covers all the territory. To apply it, first identify and discuss the primarily physical or sensuous elements of your topic, the three-dimensional, concrete realities. Then move on, in any order, to its emotional overtones, its mental ramifications, and its spiritual implications. These aspects may well overlap, of course, but it will be truly surprising if this grid can't help you develop a pattern for your material.

The Straw Man

One time-honored if slightly unprincipled way to build up your own argument is to start out by demolishing that of a fictitious (and slightly inferior) opponent, usually an argument that you borrow or adapt from the position of a real adversary. For example, let's say you're a physician and you're angry about the refusal of the administration of the hospital where you work to plan for expansion, though its facilities are dreadfully overcrowded. You might begin your argument by saying something like this: "Those who feel that high-quality patient care can be offered in the corridors of a major metropolitan hospital are in for a series of rude shocks and not a few lawsuits." Or you might want to tone it down slightly and make a more sober, dramatic appeal: "Three days ago a young mother, a patient of mine, nearly lost her child and possibly her life when her gurney could not be wheeled past the crowd of pre-op patients lined up in the corridor outside Surgery C. Those who urge us to forego expanding this hospital will be responsible when a patient *does* die because of the overcrowding here."

In both cases, as you can see, this writer begins by pointing a critical finger at an opposing group who appears to be urging that the hospital stop expanding. Whether this group actually feels this way or not is beside the point; the writer gets a running jump into his own argument (and appeals to the reader's sympathy at the same time) by ricocheting off the point of view he ascribes to his opponents.

Handle this technique with care, because it can backfire. Don't be too sarcastic or ridicule your opponent. Readers are put off, rather than warmed up to your point of view, if you're too caustic or vindictive. The major virtue of this technique is that it gives you a point of departure from which to start organizing your material.

5

Writing the Rough Draft

As YOU begin the rough draft, you face the most demanding stage of the writing process: getting a coherent sequence of words, sentences, and paragraphs down on paper. Even after you've prepared to write and have chosen a tentative organization for your material, this stage is often the most frustrating. The relatively secure stage of lists and other organizational strategies is over. Now you're faced with the writing itself. And you can't imagine how those neat outlines will ever become clean, straightforward exposition.

At the draft writing stage, the tendency to procrastinate becomes most overwhelming. As you sit before the blank page, with your index cards and outlines strewn around you, pen posed to write, panic begins to mount. Your thoughts range from the jumbled to the hysterical. Tension makes your neck and shoulders ache and your stomach tighten. The impulse to get up, to escape from the claustrophic prison of the writing setting becomes irresistible: You pace the floor and find unnecessary errands to run or telephone calls to make. Fear. Headaches. Too much coffee.

If you *are* able to get a few words down on the page, you can't sustain the flow. You've rewritten the first two sentences dozens of times, and the floor around your desk is littered with the crumpled evidence of your false starts.

Calm yourself. Remember, you've successfully laid the groundwork for this stage, and that preparation has included various forms of *actual writing*—not of drafts, admittedly, but of notes, lists, profiles, outlines, and log entries. The thoughts are there, the material is there, the interest and planning are there, you know you are capable of forming letters and words. Now all you have to do is carry the process one step further.

"Convince yourself that you are working in clay not marble, on paper not eternal bronze: let that first sentence be as stupid as it wishes. No one will rush out and print it as it stands. Just put it down; then another. Your whole first paragraph or first page may have to be guillotined in any case after your piece is finished: it is a kind of forebirth."

— JACQUES BARZUN

It may help to remind yourself that the process is still provisional. This is only a *rough* draft; it will inevitably need further revision. There will be other drafts. You will have time to change your mind, vary a phrase, rework the first sentence or page if you wish. But the essence here is to get something down on paper—knowing that you may change it later. Ignore the voice of the internal critic, who would halt the flow of words and have you obsessively trying to find the *mot juste*. He will soon become useful, when you enter into the final stage of the process—revising the draft that you produce now. But for the time being, tune him out.

Because we have found that blocked writers are often still conceptually stumped, unclear about where their ideas are taking them even at this middle stage of the writing process, we recommend that you return to your Purpose Statement once more. Then cover some basic techniques (presented in this chapter), such as the Sensory Monologue or Waxing Nostalgic, used just to get the pen moving across the page. This gives you the opportunity to focus on an unrelated subject momentarily—one that you always have some thoughts on—and to write about it before returning to your primary subject with less tension and less fear.

Once you've thawed out a bit on a simple task, we suggest ways, such as the Nonstop, to apply your newly recovered writing fluency to the topic at hand. And once we've gotten you started writing on your topic, we want to keep you at it until you've completed the draft. The remainder of this chapter, then, helps you sustain the flow of words, using techniques such as rewarding yourself, changing your writing tools or your point of view, and learning to jump constructively from job to job without losing momentum.

Read through all the techniques we describe in this section and find those that pertain most closely to your blocking experience. And use these techniques flexibly. You may find that one of them works for you immediately. If so, keep on using it. But if the first one doesn't work, try the second, the third, and so on. And try them more than once. As the writing process unfolds and your moods and attitudes change at different times with different jobs, you will have varying degrees of unblocking success with the same technique.

At some point in the process, all writers, blocked or not, find that they have to call on the oldest motivating method known to humanity: sheer willpower. They have to just sit down at the desk, take pen in hand, and begin. That's all there is to it. Just the writer, the page, and a sense of commitment. No tricks, no mirrors, no hocus-pocus. It sometimes takes a lot of grit and dedication to pull yourself together when you're blocking badly, but the experience of mastering your hesitation is self-reinforcing: The more often you succeed, the easier it gets.

Getting Started . . .

REVIST YOUR PURPOSE STATEMENT

Before you even try to begin the draft, refer back once more to your Purpose Statement. Remember that as you gain more familiarity with the job, your sense of purpose may change. And more than once. In thinking about your subject, in researching it, talking about it, in developing your organizational framework for it, you may lose your original orientation toward it. This is natural. It's a sign that your work to that point has been productive and is leading to more advanced insights.

Keep articulating these changes by writing them out as Purpose Statements as you move through the process, so that you can always orient yourself toward a goal. We have seen far more writing projects delayed and botched because their originators *under*defined their goals than because they *over*-defined them. According to James Adams,

> Difficulty in isolating the problem is often due to the tendency to spend a minimum of effort on problem-definition in order to get to the important matter of solving it. Inadequately defining the problem is a ten-

dency that is downright foolish on an important and extensive problem-solving task. A relatively small amount of time spent in carefully isolating and defining the problem can be extremely valuable . . . in illuminating possible simple solutions.

REVISIT YOUR SENTENCE OUTLINE

As a final step in reconnecting with your Purpose Statement, go back to the Sentence Outline that you developed in the last section. Notice again how the central idea of your Purpose Statement breaks down into a series of ordered and ranked subordinate ideas. Here you can see that on a conceptual level, at least, all is certainly not a vacuum. You have not only a destination, but also a map of the way to get there. Now you simply need to follow your own directions.

Take it a step at a time and treat each sentence on the outline separately when you write, using it as a point of departure for draft sections or for new notes, lists, and outlines. As you work to flesh out the conceptual structure of your outline, you may occasionally hit a special kind of snag: You're clear about sentences I.A. through I.C., say, under the first heading on your outline. However, you're not so sure about II.A. You feel a little uneasy when you reread it. Is it truly what you meant to say? Or does it need more work, more analysis, more thinking through? Don't let this mild doubt block you. Instead, use Cooker Sheets to work out your problem.

COOKER SHEETS

Cooker Sheets are a way of recording on the page the self-interrogation process that goes on when you try to investigate and clarify your views on a particular subject. Because this method lets you work through thought processes on the page in black and white, it lets you see in detail, as though under a microscope, the strengths and weaknesses of your conceptual processes.

Cooker Sheets can be used at any place in the writing process. Here's how they work: Start by writing your subject, a subordinate thought, an outline entry, a key word or phrase, or the conceptual problem you're working on at the top of a blank page. Then divide the sheet horizontally into approximate thirds. Label the top third *First Thoughts*, the second third *Queries*, and the bottom third *New Directions*. Under these headings you will record the pattern of your mental inquiry as it moves from initial impulse to critical reaction to final synthesis of the first two.

Begin by jotting down on the upper third of the page everything that comes to mind (or out of your notes) about your topic, without bothering to rank or order the ideas. Set a three-minute time limit for this stage. When your time is up, take a short break to let your first thoughts incubate a little before your return to the Cooker Sheet.

Then reread what you've written and immediately respond to it in the *Queries* space. Now you're conducting an interview with yourself, looking for new angles and weak spots. The first entries are like free associations, the second are your reactions to them.

Continue directly on to the third section. Usually the creative interaction between the first two sections will have already given you ideas about what your next steps should be: further research, redirection of your views, rephrasing, a decision to delete something or include it elsewhere, or even the beginnings of a rough draft.

Here's an example of how one student used the Cooker Sheet technique to work from clichés to her own ideas on the topic of working women:

SUBJECT:
Working wives: Don't their husbands resent it?

FIRST THOUGHTS:

They don't get elaborate meals.

The house isn't as neat.

They have to run their own errands.

They have to listen to their wife's complaints instead of just unloading theirs on her.

They have to readjust their vacations to suit her schedule.

They contribute a lot more money for eating out.

QUERIES:

Are elaborate meals and spotless houses that important?

Is readjusting vacations and helping to pay for meals out, etc., a high price to pay for the benefits of a second paycheck?

Can errands be shared so that no one gets stuck with doing them all?

Can complaints also be shared equally?

NEW DIRECTIONS:

A husband may sacrifice some comforts and advantages when his wife goes to work, but compared to the benefits, both financial and psychological, the disadvantages look pretty trivial.

The notes on this Cooker Sheet helped the writer to feel more positive about her subject, so that she was able to begin her first draft. When you're starting a writing project, be alert to positive feelings so that you can recognize a surge of creativity.

SEIZE THE CREATIVE MOMENT

When the muse decides to visit, drop everything else and be as hospitable as possible. Don't let anyone or anything else interrupt. Let the phone ring or the dinner burn. If you're getting ready for bed, put a robe on and make a cup of tea:

You're about to stay up late. Of all the techniques designed to help you write, the most reliable is simply to take full advantage of your own burst of native inspiration whenever it appears.

"I have just spent a good week, alone like a hermit, and as calm as a god. I abandoned myself to a frenzy of literature; I got up at midday, I went to bed at four in the morning. I dined with Dakno; I smoked fifteen pipes in a day; I have written eight *pages."*

— GUSTAVE FLAUBERT

What does a "creative moment" feel like? You'll have no trouble recognizing it, even if you've never thought of it that way before. You've had them often, usually at the wrong moment, the most awkward, inconvenient occasion imaginable: in the middle of the night when you're sound asleep, while you're trying to settle a conflict with your lover, or as you're about to deliver a few well-chosen remarks on production to the corporate vice-president.

Usually there's a flash of insight into a problem you've been grappling with for days. And it's often completely unrelated to whatever is going on around you at the moment. There's a good reason for this: Your unconscious is helping you out by taking the problem on and working on it when your conscious mind is directed at what's happening in the environment around you. Since the unconscious never quits working, it will pursue a solution even when you're doing something else, like sleeping.

In fact, messages from your conscious mind about the problem can even obstruct the creative operation of the unconscious, so it's often best to distract yourself deliberately for a while when you feel dried up, bored, weary—to think of something else so that the unconscious can function unobstructed. As physicist J. Robert Oppenheimer puts it: "Theoretical insights flourish best when the thinker is apparently wasting time." Suddenly—bang!—in the middle of a long putt, sautéeing chicken, taking a shower, or a snooze on the couch, the answer will leap forth. When it does, drop everything else and go to work. Better to be considered a little eccentric on occasion than to stare at a blank page for hours.

FROSTING FIRST

No one will ever know, or care, that you wrote the last paragraph first and only tacked on the introduction after the rest of the draft was written. When you're faced with a long report, proposal, or paper, give yourself a break: Pick the

---

"Too often I wait for the sentence to finish taking shape in my mind before setting it down. It is better to seize it by the end that first offers itself, head or foot, though not knowing the rest, then pull: the rest will follow along."

— ANDRÉ GIDE

---

easiest, most interesting, or most fully understood place to begin, just to get started. The idea is to get *anything* down on the page (maybe even a doodle) so that its blankness will no longer be so terrifying. It works.

When you have one section written, you'll find it easier to continue. And you can always rearrange the parts and add smooth transitions later. If you're not sure how to find the easiest place to start, try doing some Nonstops, which we discuss soon.

SENSORY MONOLOGUE

The feeling of absolute empty-headedness that typifies severe blocking is something of an illusion. The mind is never completely still, even when we sleep, and when we're awake and alert, there's plenty going on in it that we can appropriate for unblocking, no matter how anxious we feel.

Perhaps the most basic level of the mind's activity is simple observation and interpretation of the data transmitted to it by our senses. If your fear is so strong that you can't yet face your topic, begin by writing about the concrete sensations you're experiencing: What do you see? Hear? Smell? How does the pen in your hand feel, or the typewriter keys under your fingertips? Are there certain parts of your body that you're especially conscious of? Describe the sensations.

Look around you. What is your environment like? Pick one aspect of it and describe it for five minutes. Use ordinary, simple words. Don't try to be profound or poetic. Just keep the pen moving across the page. Your only task is to be as descriptive and fluid as possible without disrupting the stream of your observations. Once you've begun to thaw out, the rough draft will be much less fearsome.

CRANK LETTER

The Crank Letter makes use of a substitution technique also known as "Kick the Dog" or "Bête Noire" (French for "black beast," i.e., pet peeve). Remember our description in Chapter 1 of Pete A., who was so enraged at the editorial hypocrisy of his local newspaper that he became obsessed with crime in the streets? The paper's hypocrisy was his *bête noire*. Had he not been crippled by his internal critic's invidious comparisons of his writing with the staff's, he might have been able to use his gripe to overcome his block. We all have our curmudgeonish sides. They can play a powerful role when we're too blocked to sidestep the fears that underlie them.

Basically, all this technique involves is turning your panic into anger at an outward object, displacing it into something or someone that functions as a surefire irritant in your life. The way it works is simple. Pick a favorite frustration, something that really bugs you (e.g., big trucks that tailgate you on the freeway, newspaper vending machines that take your money but don't give you a paper, people who nudge you with their carts in the supermarket line). Write a virulent blast about it. Address the letter to the president / editor-in-chief / mayor / chairman of the board / congressman or anyone in authority. Feel free to be as nasty as you please. No one will ever see the letter. Once it's written, it's already served its purpose. You'll reread it, laugh or grimace, and toss it in the wastebasket. Having vented your spleen on a substitute frustration, you'll be ready to go to work.

WAXING NOSTALGIC

Another personal resource that can be used to trigger writing when you're blocking on your task is your own infinite pool of memories. Pick one that is especially vivid and detail all its sights, sounds, smells, tastes, textures, thoughts, hopes, fears, and other associations in writing. Often this kind of memory method works best immediately after you've completed a Systematic Relaxation exercise, when relaxation helps open you up to vivid fantasies. In fact, you may want to use the scene that you selected for the Intentional Imagery relaxation technique in the prewriting section. These scenes are usually very well suited for use in getting the draft under way, as long as they are based on personal memory.

Usually you'll find that describing one memory in this detailed way naturally leads to descriptions of others. Go ahead and indulge the impulse to move from one scene to another, dwelling on each only long enough to jot down its highlights. The point, again, is to get words flowing onto the page, using anything that helps you do this when you're blocking.

HARNESSED DAYDREAMS

Been gazing out the window a lot lately, wishing that you were anywhere else but at this infernal desk with this same insolent sheet of paper staring back at you blankly? Keep it up. You may be able to turn your susceptibility to visual distraction to your advantage.

Imagery, as we mentioned, can be an effective way to get words flowing. Producing a vivid scene in your mind can give you all the detail and drive needed to get you started and keep the prose moving once you're well into your material.

INTERVIEWER: *"How did* The Sound and the Fury *begin?"*

FAULKNER: *"It began with a mental picture. I didn't realize at the time it was symbolical. The picture was of the muddy seat of a little girl's drawers in a pear tree, where she could see through a window where her grandmother's funeral was taking place and report what was happening to her brothers on the ground below."*

Try letting the subject of your actual task suggest the scene. Reread your notes or look over what you've written so far, then close your eyes or stare out the window. Pay attention to what comes to mind. If it's unclear or not as pertinent to the topic as you'd like, exercise a little editorial redirection and guide it gently but firmly toward more relevant areas. Then just start recording on paper, in detail, what you see in your mind's eye. The efficacy of this technique in helping start a stopped writer will surprise you.

NONSTOPS (KITCHEN-SINKING IT)

Now that you feel comfortable enough with yourself, your

setting, and your tools so that you can write smoothly about an unrelated subject, we'd like to help you turn your newly regained capability toward writing about your topic. Having reassured yourself that you still have the means, now you need to apply it to the task at hand.

A good way to start a draft rolling is to use a Nonstop. Give yourself a specific time limit—from five to fifteen minutes—and the command to keep your pen constantly moving across the page for the entire time period. With nonstop writing you set up a highly auspicious, nearly fail-safe situation for getting something on your topic down on the page. You also effectively push aside your internal critic by not giving yourself the time to stop and make judgments as you write.

Nonstops are part warm-up, part free association, and mostly a trial run in which you directly confront and explore whatever may be intruding into your concentration and disrupting your ability to write about your topic. Nonstops should be playful. They help you work through feelings that would otherwise distort or too narrowly channel your thoughts, and they help you discover the right words, the best stance toward your subject.

If you fear that what you put on the page will be too

". . . the two documents I speak of were based upon, and extracted from such a preliminary private outpouring. But this latter voluminous effusion is, ever, so extremely familiar, confidential and intimate—in the form of an interminable garrulous letter addressed to my own fond fancy—that, though I always, for easy reference, have it carefully typed, it isn't a thing I would willingly expose to any eye but my own. And even then, sometimes I shrink."

— HENRY JAMES

---

clumsy, awkward, or intimate to bear revealing, remind yourself that no one else will ever see what you write, so you can afford to write anything you want. Throw it all in, including the proverbial kitchen sink. Then if you later find that it truly is garbage, you can always junk it. (You'll find, however, that your Nonstops are never as threatening as you fear. In fact, you'll probably reveal to yourself—and even purge—some of the anxieties that are contributing to your block in the first place.)

The ground rules for doing a Nonstop are simple. You write about anything and everything that comes to mind, whether it's about the topic, the blocking experience, or the man in the moon. Give your mind license to take you wherever it wants. And to keep the internal critic at bay while you Nonstop, put your notes, lists, and outlines away. Clear the desk for action. The only unbreakable rule is, keep moving the pen across the page or punching the keys or talking into the tape recorder (see our next technique) until your time is up. DON'T STOP!!

Here's how journal-keeping expert Tristine Rainer, author of *The New Diary*, describes the basic Nonstop technique, which she calls "Free-Intuitive Writing":

> You relax and try to empty your mind. You don't think about anything. You simply wait for whatever comes into your mind, and you write it just as it comes, without worrying about whether it makes sense. You let your hand do the writing. You record what you hear from the back of your mind. Nothing is irrelevant. You try to capture every word and image that occurs to you. It may all seem silly, just nonsense, but you write it anyway. It may seem embarrassing, but you write it anyway. You write fast, so fast that you don't have time to think about what you are doing. You don't take time to censor or make sense . . .
>
> . . . You might avoid looking at the page entirely as you are writing or close your eyes. You can ignore all

rules of punctuation, capitalization, grammar, and logical meaning. You can begin arbitrarily with any letter, such as "I" and then write quickly, in a semitrancelike state. If you find yourself thinking or trying to make sense, you can stop writing, try to relax completely, and wait for the conscious effort to subside. If you sense a break [or block] in the flow of intuitive writing you can repeat the last spontaneous word (for example, "station station station") until the nonlogical language reasserts itself.

You needn't quit after one Nonstop. Try several. Each one will release more creative juices and come closer to saying what you want to say. And knowing in advance that you'll try more than one Nonstop will give you license to run with the thought on the page without feeling the resistance that comes when you feel as though you're stuck with only one chance.

When you've finished, you can stop briefly to reread what you've written, but don't revise, reorganize, or worry about punctuation, spelling, and grammar at this point. You're giving yourself permission to write carelessly. You won't like everything you've written in a Nonstop, but you will invariably uncover enough good material to fuel further writing.

Here's an example of how one student used a five-minute Nonstop to begin drafting an English assignment:

There must be some way to write about this but I sure don't know what it is. It seems like such a dumb subject, write about what you can see in front of you. Oh well, I guess I better start. Really, the problem is that I am completely bored. I mean everyone writes about the fog coming down from the mountain. It seems so ridiculous. How could I describe that in a way that is interesting. Ho hum. Well, let's see. There's the fog. And it's moving. And there are some trees sticking up through it. And they are growing on a mountain. I feel like a complete idiot. I better be more poetic. Fog is sailing through the trees down the mountain slope. That sounds a little better. But what about some embellishment?

Novelist, playwright, and creative writing instructor Sid Stebel has for years successfully applied a Nonstopping technique to his work. Stebel's system is extremely simple. In the morning, in his usual writing environment, he puts pen to paper and writes at top speed, putting whatever comes into his head down on paper. And when he says "whatever," he means just that. One word triggers another. His mind leaps from irrelevancy to irrelevancy. The process is highly chaotic and nonrational, but highly productive also. As he told us recently,

> What's important about what we have to offer is what's in our unconscious. My system is really a way to get in touch with your unconscious, on the theory that it really will provide more grist for your mill, more original ideas, and more important, will provide more material that you are emotionally hung up on.... Therefore the material might tend to be more powerful.

When the creative burst comes to a natural halt—and it always does—he makes no attempt to revise or edit what's on paper. (Usually he has anywhere from two to five or more pages at this stage.) In fact, and he emphasizes this point, he *never* rereads what he's just written without first setting it aside for awhile.

After at least a week in his case, sometimes longer, Stebel goes back to his Nonstop, takes red pencil in hand, and begins reading it. As he goes, he circles words or phrases that tug at his attention, that seem to jump up off the page at him. These are messages from his unconscious. They form the earliest core of a developing piece. Identifying them is the heart of the first stage of Stebel's method.

The second stage is a duplicate of the first, except that this time Stebel uses the words that he's circled on his first draft as mental triggers. Again, he puts down anything that comes to mind in response to these signals. And again, when he's done he puts the draft away and does not reread it until a week or so later.

He repeats the cycle until links begin to form between circled phrases and words. A story begins to emerge. And the rest is more or less a matter of filling in the blanks. The process has worked so well that "Today," he says, "I have more ideas for novels, plays, and articles than I can possibly finish in a lifetime."

Talk It Into A Tape Recorder

Many people are better talkers than writers—speech is more natural and much less intimidating for them than the written word. If this sounds like you, there is a way to capitalize on your predisposition: Try talking your rough draft (or Nonstop) into a tape recorder.

"Raymond Chandler and I discussed this once, and he admitted to the most bitter reluctance to commit anything to paper. He evolved the following scheme: He had a tape recorder into which he spoke the utmost nonsense—a stream of consciousness which was then transcribed by a secretary and which he then used as a basis for his first rough draft. Very laborious. He strongly advised me to do the same . . . in fact became so excited that he kept plying me with information for months about the machine that helped him."

— S. J. PERELMAN

If you try this approach, remember not to worry about grammar and organization. What you may lose in careful construction you will gain in naturalness and liveliness. You will find that you can cover much more ground by talking; it's simply faster and easier than writing. Just remember not to censor or criticize yourself as you talk—this is still not the time for your internal critic's comments. Don't worry about being repetitive or interrupting yourself either. If you suddenly recall an important point you want to include elsewhere, just say it immediately and decide where to put it later, after everything else is on tape. (Putting extraneous remarks and reminders right there in the flow of the narrative is an unblocking technique in itself.)

There is one drawback to using tape: You have to transcribe it onto paper before you can work with it in the revision stage. Transcription can be a tedious and expensive process, but for those who get a usable rough draft and relief from writer's block, the expense is unquestionably worth it.

...Keeping the Flow Going

SIGNPOSTS

It's natural to run out of steam before you've gotten as far along as you'd like, especially when you're working on a long job. Don't push yourself to continue when you're feeling exhausted. Before you quit, however, plant a booster in the

---

"As soon as a piece of work is out of hand and before going to sleep, I like to begin another; it may be to write only half-a-dozen lines; but that is something towards Number the Next."

— WILLIAM MAKEPEACE THACKERAY

---

text—a Signpost for the next writing session. Leave off with directions to yourself about what should come next. Write down a phrase, a word, or better yet, a complete sentence to lead you back into the mainstream of the writing process.

Whenever possible, try not to begin a writing session facing a blank page. Even if you decide to ignore the booster you've planted, seeing it there will be comforting. It will give you something concrete to react to instead of inviting emptiness, panic, and blocking to set in.

THE BREADCRUMBS STRATEGY

The Breadcrumbs Strategy, originated of course by Hansel and Gretel, works like this: Successful draft writing means that at some point you inevitably become so involved with your topic and the flow of your thoughts that the mundane demands of daily life—appointments, grocery shopping, getting your laundry—begin to fade into the mental woodwork. And so they should. But unless you record them somewhere, you won't be able to quite forget them while you work. Instead of fading completely and graciously as they should, they'll resurface again and again in the back of your mind to haunt you until you've safely written them down (or taped them) in a place where they can easily be retrieved.

And this same kind of distraction can result from extraneous thoughts about the topic and about your draft. As you're working on the conclusion, a great lead may occur to you. Or you'll recall a knotty conceptual problem or factual issue that needs more researching. You need to keep track of these vagrant promptings while you defer the more difficult chores and keep the words flowing.

The way to do this is to go ahead and write notes, thoughts, instructions to yourself—i.e., Breadcrumbs—either on the draft itself, or on a separate sheet of paper kept handy for just this purpose. After all, it's only a draft. And it's usually not one that you have to show to anyone else. Use the margins for these jottings. Or insert them in brackets right in the text itself [like this]. When you've vanquished the wicked old blocking witch for the day, you can still find your way back out of the forest . . . and go pick up your clean shirts.

CREATIVE JUGGLING

As anyone who must write regularly knows all too well, it's an unheard-of luxury to have enough time for a writing project so that you can start and finish it, from first vague concept to final revision, without countless interruptions. For the professional, the businessperson, the writer of technical material, the student, and even the committed amateur journalist, writing is nearly always done against tight deadlines. Projects always overlap. And they always take longer to finish than the writer expects, no matter how experienced he or she may be.

Creative Juggling helps you make the best use of your time by preventing the useless obsessiveness that goes on in your mind when you hit a snag in your writing. Instead of just sitting there paralyzed, while your mind runs around and around in an ever-deepening rut, you can give yourself a work break by picking up part of another job. A brief recess away from the task that you're blocking on, even time spent working at something equally demanding, will usually let you come back with a fresh perspective and a new angle of attack.

Creative Juggling can also result from an outburst of inspiration. Just as you're beginning to weary of drafting the mid-section of the annual report, you have a brilliant insight into how to recast the opening sentence of that press release you've been struggling with.

In short, try to be opportunistic about your block. Take advantage of the fragmentation and chaos that it seems to cause you. When your mind wants to skitter away from one project, push it in a constructive direction, toward another. Shift from a demanding mental task to a routine mechanical one, from pulling the best introduction for Project A out of your head to typing up your notes for Project C. Skip around, adding a few notes to the manuscript, a page or two to the press release, and a last rereading to a memo. Apply the same technique to individual projects, especially long ones, by jumping from one segment to another.

"I can write rapidly for a while, then there come stages where I'm stuck, and I might spend an hour on a page. But that's rather rare, because when I find I'm being bogged down, I will skip a difficult part and go on, you see, and come back to it fresh another day."

— HENRY MILLER

You may feel uncomfortable about setting something aside when you're blocking, as though you're running away. You're not. It's not cowardice or irresponsibility. Instead, we see it as artful juggling and as a skillful use of incubation.

REWARD YOURSELF

At appropriate points in the process, perhaps as you finish each writing session or each page, give yourself a gift. It needn't be elaborate. Use a simple reward, like a short walk, a few minutes of listening to a favorite record or tape, something good to eat, a chat with a friend—any of the countless small pleasures in life. If you're working in an office, plan a lunch or dinner break, or a late-afternoon pause for a cup of coffee or a glass of wine, as your reward for a job well done.

If you're working on a long project, don't wait until it's finished before you reward yourself. Psychologists feel that positive reinforcement works best when it comes at frequent intervals, immediately after you've completed each task.

REREAD WHAT YOU'VE WRITTEN

When you've been away from the work for a while or when you're feeling stuck, another effective way to refresh your motivation is by simply rereading what you've written. Merely looking over what you've managed to accomplish proves you can do it; you can forge ahead and repeat the feat.

Don't revise or criticize at this point; premature revision is a surefire way to sabotage your momentum. You can spend all your time rewriting the first page. Remember, the critical function has no place in the first three stages of the writing process—wait until the fullest, though rough, expression of the idea is complete. So try to limit yourself to reading to get a sense of what you've done so far, where you've gotten, and what needs to come next.

If you can't resist the impulse to change your work, avoid marking up the draft itself. Make notes on a separate piece of paper, keyed to the draft by page number. Then put

---

"I always begin my task by reading the work of the day before, an operation which would take me half an hour, and which consisted chiefly in weighing with my ear the sound of the words and phrases . . . by reading what he has last written, just before he recommences his task, the writer will catch the tone and spirit of what he is then saying, and will avoid the fault of seeming to be unlike himself."

— ANTHONY TROLLOPE

---

these notes aside, knowing that you'll come back to them once you have finished the first draft.

THE PAST-SUCCESS SPRINGBOARD

As many of our writing friends assure us, when they're really blocked they tend to "see the rose through world-colored glasses," to borrow Mort Sahl's trenchant line. A depressing pall, like a thick dirty-gray fog, settles inside their heads. They feel as though their verbal days are numbered.

As tricky and difficult as it is to pull yourself out of a writing slump, we all have plenty of internal tools on hand to do so. An important one is the memory of your own past successes.

Start by declaring firmly to yourself, out loud if possible, that you're not going to let your own fear defeat you. Now repeat it. Say it like you mean it. Listen to yourself say it. You know you've managed to write well before and you intend to do so again. Remind yourself that blocking is never permanent, and that the mood you're in at the moment is only one of the many moods that are a part of life. There is also joy, vitality, and excitement—all of which you can expect to re-experience soon.

Telling yourself all this won't, of course, miraculously clear up your block right there on the spot, but it will make you receptive to an uplift in your mood. Recent psychological studies confirm the effect of this kind of positive self-suggestion techniques: If you tell yourself that you're resourceful and capable, you will become more so, and the blocking struggle will begin to fade.

The next step is to reinforce your positive self-talk with concrete proof that you really *do* know your job. Go back through your files, rummage through your drawers and shelves, and pick out a few past examples of your work, those that you know are good and that you're especially proud of. Reread a successful paper, report, or letter. (This is another reason to keep a Treasury—for just these moments of brief despair.)

Try to bring to mind as clearly as possible how you went about creating a successful piece of writing. Remember that you struggled, even then, to find the right words, that you made false starts, and that you restructured the work even after you thought you had a final draft. If you were blocked then too, try to recall what it was that helped you get going. Maybe a casual chat with a friend helped you articulate your concepts and get past your hesitation, or maybe it was just taking a brief break from the job so that your thoughts could incubate. Whatever it was, ultimately it worked. And the evidence is right there before your eyes.

FRESH SLANT, FRESH FORMAT

Sometimes you grind to a halt in the middle of the writing process just because you've lost your sense of excitement and originality about the job. You've worked through some of the earlier problems with getting yourself ready to write and you've done a lot of research and organizing—you're even well along into the rough draft—but the material now seems cold, mechanical, and dull to you, and the work has become just another routine, plodding chore. In short, you're bored.

This isn't the worst kind of block to have. In many cases, sheer dogged perserverance may be sufficient to overcome boredom; if you can muster the willpower to put down one word after another, the job will eventually be completed. And upon review, it may even turn interesting once again.

But there are also effective ways to liven up a task that has become boring by changing the way you view the material, by addressing it to a different reader, or by just changing the format.

For example, consider writing a letter in the form of a memo, a report in a question-and-answer format, or a term paper in the form of a fairy tale ("Once upon a time there were three macroeconomic theories . . ."). Or try one of the alternatives we discuss below.

"Tom Wolfe, totally blocked on his first famous article, a story about customized cars for Esquire, *wrote a really socko memorandum to his editor on the subject. The editor ran the memo as the article. Wolfe now writes all his articles as memos."*

— TIME, *October 3, 1977, p. 101*

Dick-and-Janing

Remember the first books of childhood, with their familiar characters and simple declarative sentences? "See Spot run. Hear Jane laugh. See Zeke rake leaves." Entire stories told in sentences of less than five words each.

When you face an especially delicate or difficult writing assignment, you can get the skeleton of a rough draft started by reducing the first few paragraphs to Dick-and-Janese. Dick-and-Janing is especially helpful for people writing on technical subjects or those who tend to get bogged down in professional and bureaucratic jargon. If you're not used to this approach, you may be surprised to see how many ideas can be expressed in this oversimplified manner.

Using your Outline and Purpose Statement, state your main ideas very briefly and sketch in the subpoints in short, overly simplistic sentences. Once you've got a draft, reread it to check the clarity of the basic pattern of your thoughts. Then rework your sentences, substituting more appropriate language, more sophisticated descriptions, and generally more advanced prose.

Even when you rephrase, keep it simple. Bear in mind that readers rarely, if ever, complain that writing is too easy to follow.

Cablese

An alternative to Dick-and-Janing is Western-Unioning. Instead of thinking of your audience as having the attention span of a six-year-old, assume that its chief characteristic is a furious impatience about getting to the heart of the message. Boil it down to as few words as possible. Make them as terse, urgent, and concise as you can. You might even try printing it out in block letters on a clean sheet of paper to see whether you've achieved your purpose.

> DEAR MR. GETAHEAD:
>   MY REPORT ON REAMCO SENT 2:12 E.S.T.
> PURCHASE ADVISED. NOTE LAST PAGE ON PROJECTED
> CAP. EXPENDS. ALSO BOARD RESHUFFLE. DEADLINE
> THURSDAY. WAITING YOUR DECISION.
>   FREDERICKS

You can apply this technique to short jobs *and* to chunks of longer jobs. Technical writers use this approach when they need to write crisp research abstracts or punchy proposal summaries.

Letter to a Friend

Even blocked writers generally find writing to a friend the easiest kind of writing to do. You know your audience well, your desire to communicate is strong and genuine, and you trust your reader's interest in what you have to say. It's easy to anticipate how a friend will respond to your letter, and his or her imagined reactions may stimulate you to be more voluble, playful, and creative.

Try working through a block on a difficult project by rewriting it as though you were starting a Letter to a Friend. Begin with the salutation at the top of the page, as usual. Use the first few lines to warm up: Gossip, get something off your chest, report the latest news. Then gradually begin discussing the writing project you're working on. And then just take it from there.

One writer used this technique to help him write a report for a particularly irascible university administrator:

> *Dear Arthur:*
>
> *I'm not sure that this is going to work, but I'm desperate enough to try anything. His nibs handed me his pet project after he totally failed to come up with a solution. We're going to have to evaluate all our courses every quarter; you know how the faculty will love that. They see evaluation as a monumental waste of time and an invasion of their privilege to conduct classes as they see fit. I suppose I'll have to start the manifesto by telling them that the evaluations will give them additional information—feedback—and should therefore help them improve their classes. Then I'll have to go on to describe the evaluation form we've drafted (actually I did it, but it'll be we in the letter, of couse) and invite their comments and additions. And I'll tell them how we plan to administer the evaluation so as to interrupt class time as little as possible.*
>
> *Amazing—I've begun to write it already. And it's not too stuffy. Thanks—I'll continue this later—right now I've got some writing to do.*
>
> *Fred*

Once the letter is completed, it's a simple matter to drop the salutation and opening sentences, flesh out the content a bit, and your letter has become a first draft.

CHANGE YOUR TOOLS

Sometimes you can reinvigorate the writing process and put yourself back on the fast track by just changing your tools. If you've been typing and you begin to feel as if there are no words left in the keys, try putting the machine aside and picking up a pen for a while. Try using a pencil, felt-tips, a ballpoint, or a fountain pen and different-colored inks. The range of writing implements and experiences that are available is endless, and with each one you'll find that your writing looks different, feels different, and conveys the meanings of your words differently. (A friend of ours feels forceful and creative when she writes with felt-tips, but she's incapacitated by #3 pencils and ballpoints.) In short, play with the purely sensuous aspects of writing, with its tactile and visual dimensions, until you've developed more than just one workable—and pleasurable—way of getting the words down on paper.

"In the revisions of Barbary Shore *I had started working in longhand; as soon as I found myself blocked on the typewriter I'd shift to longhand. By the time I got to* The Deer Park *I was writing in longhand all the time. I'd write in longhand in the morning, and type up what I'd written in the afternoon."*

— NORMAN MAILER

6

Revising and Polishing

UST as you've finished getting something down on paper, at your moment of greatest relief and exhaustion, you realize that you're not quite done yet. You still have to look it over at least once more, check it, review it, and revise it if necessary. You sigh, you groan, you long for genuine respite, however brief. A perfectly normal reaction: As exhilarating as writing can be when you're free from blocks and working well, it is also draining because the only way to do it right is to truly invest yourself in it. But

---

"I can't understand how anyone can write without rewriting everything over and over again. I scarcely ever re-read my published writings, but if by chance I come across a page, it always strikes me: All this must be rewritten; this is how I should have written it."

— TOLSTOY

---

then you naturally and inevitably resist changing what you've written because, having thoroughly identified with it, you feel that change implies imperfection and criticism of you and your work.

Yet, as we've repeated time and again, all successful writers have to learn that writing is essentially rewriting. And in order to rewrite successfully you must be able to disengage yourself from the work. As artist/psychologist Dr. Safán-Gerard puts it:

> When the work is done, the creative person must be able to disrupt his oneness with the work; to stand back and assess coolly what has happened. Few people associate the joys of creativity with these self-confrontations, but they are a vital part of creation. If we are too involved in the product, editing becomes excessively painful. By washing over part of our painting, deleting several nice-sounding paragraphs, or eliminating a pet idea from a report, we feel that we are eliminating a part of ourselves. But while involvement in what we do is essential to creativity, we must also be detached enough to assess whether what we have done is fitting.

The revision stage of the writing process is finally the place to bring in the internal critic—though we must still be careful to restrain him from becoming overly obstructive; we want only *constructive* criticism at this point. Up to now, you've intentionally pushed your critic aside so that you could fully tap your creative resources and get your ideas down on paper. The revision stage, however, is really the critic's proper domain, since now you need cool assessment of your prose from a detached, analytical point of view.

So make your internal critic into an ally now. Enlist and capitalize on the highly rational perspective that he represents; put him to work pointing out the weak spots, redundancies, and ambiguities in your writing.

Because revision demands the toughest kind of self-confrontation, blocking at this last stage of the writing process has a character all its own. People who breeze through some or all of the previous steps of preparing, organizing, and draft writing may suddenly find themselves solidly blocked here. It always comes as an especially bitter and shocking surprise to reach this stage triumphantly and then find that you can't bear even to think of pressing on.

"I've made it a practice to do all my first drafts on the backs of circulars or old correspondence or something like that so I can't submit them. Then I revise, as often as necessary. When I find I'm having trouble now I'll put an old manuscript in the typewriter and just do rough drafts for awhile on the back as roughly and crudely as necessary. Then I go back and rewrite that part. That seems to have kept me from any prolonged blocks in the last few years. Nobody's going to see it but me, and I suspend criticism. I just plunge ahead and put down whatever occurs to me. Sometimes I just outline a whole paragraph . . . whatever possible avenue occurs to me I put down on paper. If that looks bad later on, I can always change it, but meanwhile I've managed to get a little further along."

— FREDERICK POHL
Noted science fiction author

Perhaps you'll feel better about revising if you remind yourself that you've already accomplished the largest and most difficult part of the writing process: You have a rough draft on paper . . . now it just needs refining. Think of revision as tinkering — essential tinkering, to be sure—but also a stage of some luxuriousness, like furnishing a house that you've just finished building.

"Rewriting is when playwriting really gets to be fun. . . . In baseball, you only get three swings and you're out. In rewriting, you get almost as many swings as you want and you know, sooner or later, you'll hit the ball."

— NEIL SIMON

Though your revision work must be as careful, detailed, and meticulous as the work you've put into every other step of the writing, it can be accomplished with a minimum of pain, anxiety, and blocking. The techniques we describe in this chapter are designed to help you do just that.

First, we recommend a series of strategies, ranging from the commonsensical one of setting the work aside for awhile and giving yourself a recess, to working at your relaxation exercise again, to altering the visual appearance of the work to make it fresher to your jaded eyes.

For the rewriting block that stems from a fear of exposing the precious yet admittedly imperfect manuscript to the critic's pitiless eye, we suggest first Reading It Out Loud, and then using a technique called Pre-empting, a way of anticipating and defusing your audience's potentially negative and critical judgments about it.

There also appears at this stage the block that results from sheer inexperience with polishing English prose. You've got the content of your idea or message down on the page, but you've got no idea how to go about making your sentences grammatically and stylistically correct. Fortunately, this is one of the simplest kinds of blocking to remedy, and we discuss a number of the basics of revision for style and accuracy at the end of this chapter.

RECESS: SET IT ASIDE AND RELAX

By the time you've finished the first draft, you're now intensely involved with the work. It is *not* likely to be easy for you to switch back quickly to the relatively impersonal, objective point of view that you need for effective revision. You already feel some resistance to subjecting your hard-won draft to criticism. Don't make it worse by trying to *force* an attitude of detachment in yourself.

Admit that you're going to have trouble seeing the forest for the trees for a while and give yourself a break. Stick the draft in a drawer or on a shelf or in your briefcase—somewhere out of sight—and do something else before you come back to it as a rewriter.

Even if this only means putting the draft of a short letter in your desk for ten minutes while you stroll down the hall to get a drink of water and chat with a friend, do it. When you come back you'll find you're now sufficiently detached from it to be able to see what needs trimming and pruning, what needs to be thinned out, and what needs to be clear cut, hauled away, and completely replanted.

USE RELAXATION STRATEGIES

The "something else" that you do when you set the draft aside might well be to practice your Systematic Relaxation technique. Tension can be a pernicious blocking cause at any stage of the writing process. You may be anxious about rereading what you've written because you've set your standards too high. You may have an especially tyrannical internal critic, one who's still not quite tamed, and who will, given the slightest opportunity to speak up again, tend to make you overly self-critical, especially now that you want to invite him back to help you correct what you've produced.

So if you find yourself tightening up at the prospect of reworking your prose, and you haven't yet incorporated a relaxation strategy into your writing process, turn back to our discussion of Systematic Relaxation approaches (i.e., Exercise, Progressive Muscle Relaxation, the Relaxation Response, Traditional Meditation, and Intentional Imagery) in Chapter 3. Experiment with the "unstressing" methods described there until you find one that permits you to approach revising in a more relaxed frame of mind.

SCHEDULE CRITICAL INPUT FROM OTHERS

Accepting someone else's criticism of your work is regarded by many blocking veterans as the most humiliating part of the whole revision process. If your job involves receiving critical feedback from others, we recommend that you protect your self-esteem by taking an active part in arranging the feedback process. Be as assertive as possible about when and how you want to receive comments and criticisms. Don't wait for "them" to decide when they will speak to you—it only adds to the indignity. Instead, suggest when and where it best suits you to hear what your supervisor or instructor has to say. This doesn't need to be done defensively, just firmly. Trust us. You will still suffer, but because you're not doing so passively, as a victim or a target, it won't sting quite so much.

PRE-EMPTING

There's nothing quite like the fear that you're facing a basically negative, skeptical, or even overtly hostile audience to turn mild hesitation into a full-blown revision block.

Deal with it like this. Go back to your Profile of the Critical Reader in the organizing section and resurrect him. Once you've gotten his image clearly established in your mind, picture him reading through your draft. Then, when he's finished, engage him in a written dialogue, one in which he takes an overtly challenging, obtuse role and questions every assertion, every point, every choice of word or phrase you've made.

Once his objections are clear, write them up into a critical review in which he attacks your work. Make it as negative as possible. Then review your draft so that you can answer his doubts effectively.

This exercise will force you to explain and illustrate your ideas, your approach, your choice of tone and diction as forcefully as possible. And by thus letting a hypothetical reader punch holes in your position, you can avoid potential weaknesses—and emphasize your strengths.

Anticipating and defusing your audience's objections in this way is known as Pre-empting. If your block stems from a fear that your reader will be indifferent to your appeal, will automatically say no, will give you a hard time, or will quibble with your logic, run through the Pre-empting exercise before you sit down to revise. Here's an example:

Suppose you're the comptroller of a large paper products corporation. You've just reviewed a request from a branch office for additional advertising funds, and you've decided to deny it. You have the power to just issue a simple "no," but you know your decision is going to be extremely unpopular, and you'd like to salvage morale as much as possible. Try writing a pre-empting dialogue, like this:

BRANCH: So, what do you think? Do we get the ad budget we want this year?

YOU: Maybe, but not this quarter.

BRANCH: What? We *need* that money! You guys at headquarters just don't know how . . .

YOU: Yes, we do. I realize how badly you need those funds, but you have to realize that the company as a whole has other needs that we feel are more important at the moment.

BRANCH: Such as?

YOU: I'll be happy to go into it in detail with you in person; but just to go over it briefly now, we have to beef up the sales force before we pour money into an ad campaign anywhere. Otherwise we create a demand that we can't respond to, potential clients don't get good service, and over the long run our image suffers. Surely you can see that.

BRANCH: Well, yes, of course I can. Look, can we get top priority for next quarter's budget?

YOU: I can't commit myself to anything right now, but I don't see why not, all things being equal. We do agree, as you know, that the need for more ad space exists in your region. Just bear with us and I think you'll see that we have your best interests at heart.

By forestalling a reader's possible doubts and objections, you come that much closer to winning him over. It's a valuable form of trouble-shooting, and a good way to undercut your fears about revising and submitting your work.

THE ARCHIVES BOX

Good revising always involves a certain amount of pruning and paring, even of those sections of the draft that you're especially proud of. Cutting these out, even when you know it's unequivocally right to do so, can be very painful, so painful that you'd rather not continue with the revision. Because you tend to identify with your writing, the act of deleting chunks of it, especially those you're particularly proud of, can feel like losing part of yourself.

There's a way to have your cake and eat it too. Indulge in this little drama of harmless but effective self-deception. Find a large, flat, page-size box and label it your Archives Box. Decorate it or wrap it in such a way (one friend of ours uses gold foil) to make the box and its contents special.

Then as you work through the revision process, put anything that you need to remove from the text but wish to preserve into the Archives Box—for posterity . . . or next week's sales report. Tell yourself that even though it's been deleted from the work at hand, it's not lost forever. Whenever you want to go back and resurrect it for another job, you can.

Not only does the Archives Box free you to make cuts objectively, it also has a secondary function. Some of those priceless bits of prose in the box may never find their way into another draft, but they can still be very useful to you if you transfer them into your Treasury file (see the prewriting section) and use them for inspiration.

CHANGE THE MEDIUM

Some degree of blocking at this final stage is due to sheer overexposure to the draft. By this point you've usually stared at the words on the page so much that you literally can't see them, at least not with a fresh, detached perspective. Here are a few ways to alter your modes of perception so that you can more readily identify the soft spots, redundancies, and other flaws in your work.

If you've written the draft out in longhand, try typing it up before you actually begin reworking it. There's something about the very appearance of words in type that casts them in a clearer light. And a typescript is easier to read than handwriting anyway. Type double- or even triple-spaced so that you'll have lots of room to make notes, shift parts of sentences around, and scribble in specific changes between the lines.

It may also sometimes be useful to reverse the process and go from typescript to longhand. Because it takes you longer to write things out, you'll find that you tend to shorten your sentences and make them much more concise. Also, because you can add and cross out more quickly, you can rework a rough section much faster with pen and paper than with typewriter.

READ IT OUT LOUD

Reading your draft aloud lets your ear pick up what your eyes may have missed. Many kinds of omissions and clumsy phrasings are best revealed orally. For example, by listening to yourself talk you'll hear a sentence that rambles on too long, awkward shifts of tone, tense, and rhythm, and paragraphs that seem too choppy. You'll notice words that are overused, not quite accurate, or ambiguous.

"Reading aloud to others my first rough draft helped to enlighten me."

— CHATEAUBRIAND

You may want to read the draft out loud to yourself first, then once again to your Friendly Ear. Having a live, sympathetic listener in front of you will enhance the value of the recitation and help distance you from the work and your fear of revision. And be sure to elicit your listener's assessment of the work's virtues as well as its failings.

Finally, it's often helpful not only to *read* the text aloud to a friend but also to explain it, to paraphrase it, line by line. We've found that this invariably helps students and clients see where the conceptual structure is still unclear, as well as discover better examples and more imaginative analogies.

LISTS

Revision is detail work, which can be intimidating because you fear that you'll miss something. You can relieve some of the pressure with checklists, devices that act like safety nets to make sure that as the writing process moves toward a conclusion, you don't stumble and fall off the tightrope by forgetting a crucial element or task.

Remember our Spoke Outlines on capital punishment in Chapter 4? Here's that student's checklist for his final draft:

- Obtain quotations from both sides—proponents and opponents of capital punishment.

- Look up statistics on the number of criminals apprehended, brought to trial, convicted, and released.

- Collect case histories of lengthy appeals, costly trials, and sentences overturned on technicalities.

- Find figures on cost per person for one year of incarceration.

- Summarize specific recommendations for changing laws and reforming the judicial system.

Use checklists to keep track of the more easily forgotten procedural matters of writing—checking facts and figures, getting signatures, obtaining permissions, researching complex ideas, looking up references and citations, inserting concrete examples to illustrate your general statements. With a complete checklist in hand, you won't have to fear you're forgetting something.

PROSE MECHANICS

Revision is the stage where you have to make the work *correct*. It has to become something that Mrs. Grundy would approve of. And that's precisely why so many people pale at this point. They can prepare, outline, and actually get the words on the page, but they feel lost when it comes to spelling, grammar, punctuation—the mechanics of writing. Commas and periods are bad enough, but when they must distinguish between restrictive and nonrestrictive clauses, they start looking for the nearest exit.

Still there is that internal critic in you just itching to get out to monkey with your prose. In fact, he probably knows more about revision than you realize. So, now is the time to let him loose. Keep him on his leash, but give him enough slack so that he can give you the benefits of his discriminating, rational intelligence, without its inhibiting drawbacks.

However painful it may sound, then, becoming familiar with the mechanical details is necessary. You don't have to master them—there are always dictionaries and reference books available. But you do need to write a passable and proper sentence, to pass successfully through the revision stage. There are standards and rules to writing, based on tradition and usage, and your readers expect your work to conform to them.

As we said in the introduction, however, this is not a grammar book. Nor is it a book about style or how to write. There are lots of excellent books available on these topics. We've listed the best in the bibliography. In particular, we'd like to urge you to read a minor classic, Strunk and White's *The Elements of Style*. And always have a good collegiate dictionary on hand.

"Writing has laws of perspective, of light and shade, just as painting does, or music. If you are born knowing them, fine. If not, learn them. Then re-arrange the rules to suit yourself."

— TRUMAN CAPOTE

There are also a few tricks of the rewriter's trade that we'd like to offer you as well. This will be by no means an exhaustive list of all the pitfalls to watch out for, but it should help assuage your worries by setting forth the more common problems that you will tend to encounter with all your first drafts. Take it slow and steady, one step at a time, and you'll find that you have less difficulty with this last stage of the writing process than you expected.

THE REVISER'S TOOLKIT

Blue-Penciling. Use a soft red or blue pencil to mark your changes—one with an eraser on the end. Write in pencil, not ink, because you will inevitably want to change your changes. Use the margins for general instructions to youself (e.g., "add example here," "tighten sentence structure," "wrong word," "cite source").

Sharpen Your Transitions. Connecting words and phrases like *although, in spite of, for example, yet, and, also,* and *first . . . second . . . third* are road signs that help your reader follow the logic of your argument. They do some of his thinking for him; since he is by definition easily distracted, these markers are essential.

Make It Concrete. Whenever possible, replace a long or abstract term *(instrument)* with a short, concrete word that appeals to the senses *(hammer)*.

"Don't write about Man, write about a man."

— E. B. WHITE

Avoid Clichés. Here's *Newsweek* writer Pete Carlson overkilling a point about clichés: "Common sense dictates, therefore, that we hold our horses. If you get rid of the cliché before we find something to replace it with, we will be opening a Pandora's box. Charging into this like a bull in a china shop would be putting the cart before the horse and creating a dangerous precedent." (Notice that Carlson also manages to mix a few metaphors in his caricature of an excessive dependence on the cliché.)

Clichés are tricky. They are terms that pass overnight

from being vivid summations of a topical point of view or attitude into mindlessly routine catchwords. Today's trendy expression is tomorrow's banality. A metaphor that seems witty one week turns stale and trite the next. The best antidote to an overdose of clichés is frequent reference to a good thesaurus of synonyms.

Avoid Jargon.   Jargon is the use of specialized terms within a well-defined professional field. It has its place. A doctor writes *PRN* on your prescription form because it's easier than writing "as needed." A computer technician talks about *downtime* because it's easier than saying "period when the computer isn't operating and can't be used because it's broken or being serviced." He or she uses the term *software* instead of saying "programs, instruction books, manuals, and so forth" for the same reason. As you can see, jargon works as a kind of shorthand so that people within a specialized field can communicate quickly and efficiently with each other.

Unfortunately, jargon is subject to abuse when it becomes a badge of status, used to differentiate an insecure minority "elite" from the "lay masses." In this guise, it's nothing more than a pretentious form of one-upmanship, whose function is to mystify, or to conceal a lack of genuine content. Any ordinary idea can be made to sound impressively arcane, for awhile anyway, if you dress it up in tinsel and glitter.

"The day is not far off when someone about to join his family will excuse himself by saying that he does not want to keep his microcluster of structured role expectations waiting."

— EDWIN NEWMAN

Use Strong Verbs. If your verbs are weak and bland, the sentence will lack life and motion. Verbs are the arteries of your prose. They move the meaning along, oxygenating and nourishing it as they go. For example, you might choose to write *slurped* instead of *drank noisily*, or *strode* instead of *walked* and your work would probably benefit. Certainly it would become more colorful.

Emphasize the active voice in your use of verb forms, but don't go overboard with it: The passive voice is occasionally quite effective. For example, you would want to use the passive form "All children should be vaccinated before they go to school" rather than the active but more awkward form "Doctors should vaccinate all children before they go to school."

Most writing, however, could stand to be made more active. Instead of saying "The exhibit was assembled by the team in two hours," this writer could have said "The team assembled the exhibit in two hours."

Another tip: Avoid transforming simple verbs, such as *applied*, *approved*, and so forth into more cumbersome noun phrases—"made an application for," or "stated their approval of"—just because you want your prose to sound more dignified. It doesn't work.

Delete Unnecessary Words. One precise word can always do the work of communication much more effectively than a cluster of words that aren't quite what you mean.

It can be exhausting to struggle patiently to find just the right word, but the results are always worth it. Making your prose concrete will also tend to make it lean and refreshingly direct.

FOR EXAMPLE:

> "Regarding the communication requested as an example of terrible writing, this paragraph is herewith enclosed."

BECOMES:

"Here's the bad writing sample you wanted."

FOR EXAMPLE:

"Our new paint additive retards the rate at which exterior surfaces reflect the ravages of time."

BECOMES:

"Our new paint additive slows peeling, chipping, and fading."

"Vigorous writing is concise. A sentence should contain no unnecessary words, a paragraph no unnecessary sentences for the same reason that a drawing should have no unnecessary lines and a machine no unnecessary parts. This requires not that the writer make all his sentences short, or that he avoid all detail and treat his subjects only in outline, but that every word tell."

— WILLIAM STRUNK

Vary Sentence Length. A sentence can be as short as one word. See? Short sentences have punch. And contemporary readers like tight, snappy prose. But. Too many. Stuck together. Can sound. Choppy. And halting.

Sentence length should vary to suit the content and tone of your material and your audience. Highly technical material, or any topic that involves a fairly complex series of conceptual links, usually benefits from shorter sentences.

But change pace now and then to keep your prose from becoming monotonous. Readers appreciate these variations. If you're writing long, complicated sentences, you'll find that you can easily cut them into smaller chunks. And conversely, if your prose is coming out in nothing but Cablese (see Chapter 5), loosen it up and add some transitional words to join the smaller segments together.

Cut and Paste.   Revision applies not only to the texture of a work—that is its words, phrases, and sentences—but also to its structure, its paragraphs, pages, and chapters. For example, you may find that a paragraph on page 2 would make a terrific opening and want to shift it forward. Or you might see that reversing the order of two paragraphs would clarify your explanation. Keep a pair of scissors and a roll of cellophane tape (we use the "magic transparent" kind) handy so that you can shift sections around as you please in your quest for a better organizational scheme.

Fit the Print to the Page.   One of the less overt tools that writers work with is the visual impression that blocks of print and white spaces make on the page. It's a subtle element of expression, but an important one, so make the impression attractive. Leave adequate margins all around the page to frame the rectangle of print. Don't use a large sheet of paper for a short note. Don't overwork visual attention-grabbers like headlines, capitalization, quotation marks, and exclamation points. Too much busy excitement on a page will only diffuse the reader's attention.

On the other hand, don't put your reader to sleep with long, unbroken paragraphs. Vary their length just as you vary your sentence lengths. When logical divisions in content occur, use headings and breaks in the flow of print to reinforce them.

THE FOG INDEX

There is a simple mechanical way to check on the readability of your prose. Called the Fog Index, it's based on the premise that shorter words and sentences tend to make easier reading, regardless of the content of the work.

Developed by Robert Gunning, The Fog Index (FI)

tells you the approximate educational level, in terms of school grades, that your reader must have attained in order to follow your meaning easily. For example, the Revised Standard Version of the *Bible* and most popular newsstand magazines have an FI of about 6, meaning that the typical sixth grader can understand them without difficulty. *Time* and *Newsweek* have FI's of about 10 (average high-school sophomore). When the FI of a piece exceeds 12 (high-school senior), it is becoming dangerously hard to read—even *Harper's* and the *Atlantic* try to maintain an FI level of between 11 and 12.

Here's how to figure the FI of any piece of writing:

1. Select a passage of consecutive sentences containing 100 words.

2. Count the number of sentences in the passage.

3. Divide the total number of words in the selection by the number of sentences. This gives you the average sentence length in words.

4. Count the words of three syllables or more in the passage. Exclude those that are capitalized, those that are combinations of short words, like *lifesaver*, and three-syllable verbs formed by adding prefixes and suffixes, like *edited* or *bellowing*. The total is the percentage of "hard" words in the selected passage.

5. Add the two totals of 3 and 4 together and multiply by 0.4—this is your FI.

The FI Test applied to a selection from *Overcoming Writing Blocks:*

1. The selected passage.
    "Just as you've finished getting something down on paper, at your moment of greatest relief and exhaustion, you realize that you're not quite done yet. You still have to look it over at least once more, check it, review it, and revise it if necessary. You sigh, you

groan, you long for genuine respite, however brief. A perfectly normal reaction: As exhilarating as writing can be when you're free from blocks and working well, it is also draining because the only way to do it right is to truly invest yourself in it. But then you naturally and inevitably resist . . ."

2. Sentence count: *5*.

3. The average sentence length in words (100 divided by 5) is *20*.

4. The number of "hard" words in passage is *10*.

5. 20 (sentence length) plus 10 (number of hard words) equals 30; 30 times 0.4 equals *12.00*. The FI for this passage is *12*, or high school-senior level.

KNOWING WHEN TO LET GO

Oddly enough, it's also possible to feel anxiety — to the extent of near hysteria — about bringing the writing process to an end, particularly when it has taken a lot of time and effort to get it moving in the first place. Going back and tinkering with the draft is essential, especially in the revision stage, but this too must ultimately come to a halt. We tend to develop a nearly parental attachment to anything we create (thus the Archive Box), fearing for its independent reception by the larger world.

The best response to this is to accept the fact that your work will never be perfect. All writing exists on a long continuum, starting with vague concepts at one end and vanishing into sublime perfection at the other. For our purposes, most of it is never destined to become the tangible realization of perfectly expressed thought and exquisitely rendered emotion that it could conceivably be. Don't fight this fact. Bring the work to life as well as you can, then release it, let it go, and go on to the next.

Part 3

Applications: Unblocking Techniques at Work

ARTS 1 and 2 of *Overcoming Writing Blocks* gave you a broad view of writing as a complex psychological and creative process and offered you dozens of techniques that can be used to overcome the difficulties that arise at each stage of the writing process. Part 3 is more specific: It shows you how to apply the unblocking techniques to distinct writing tasks.

These techniques are used successfully by professional writers—as the quotes in the text clearly show—but we focus on the needs of others who must write in order to satisfy the demands of their jobs or the need for communication. We've broken the applications down into four fairly distinct categories of writing: business, student, technical/academic/professional, and personal. Each of these categories is treated according to the demands placed upon the writer most frequently.

When we talk about *business* writers, we mean anyone in any type of business at any level: clerks, salespeople, board chairmen, administrative assistants, claims adjusters, ad agency executives, public relations people, building contractors, movie producers, manufacturers' representatives, editors, florists, pharmacists, music shop managers, bookkeepers . . . the list is endless. By and large, they work in profit-oriented environments, and they or their managers are sensitive to the fact that time is money, so the pressure to work fast always looms.

The writing these people do usually involves memos, letters, reports, proposals, occasional promotional writing (such as sales brochures), and publicity writing (such as press releases and news articles).

Students, another major group of block-prone writers, face three kinds of writing demands: essays written in an hour or two, usually in class, papers (or "themes") that may take anywhere from a few days to a week or more to write, and long-term research papers, theses, and dissertations.

The third group, technical/academic/professional

writers, generally work on what may loosely be called "research." Here we're referring to a group that tends to be more science- or social-science-oriented than those we included in the business category. This classification includes most professionals, such as engineers, computer programmers, physicists, microbiologists, architects, doctors, accountants, economists, dentists, sociologists, lawyers, chiropodists, psychologists, professors, teachers, and so forth. Although some of these individuals also work in profit-oriented firms, many can be found in nonprofit, research-oriented environments such as universities, hospitals, research institutes, and government service. Typically a technical/academic/professional writer finds himself or herself writing a journal article, an abstract, a research report, or a grant proposal.

Personal writing, our fourth category, is something of a catchall label: It includes the kind of casual but sometimes very important writing that all of us need to do occasionally. We sit down to compose a thank-you note or a greeting to a sick friend. We write a feature article for our church newsletter, fire off a blistering consumer complaint to a product manufacturer, or pull together a pithy letter to the editor of the local paper. Once in a while we may write up a resumé or brief biography as part of an application form.

Unlike business, student, and technical/academic/professional writing, personal writing isn't always a necessity. Writing a greeting card usually isn't as essential as the writing tasks required to hold down a job, run a corporation, report the results of a research study, or get a degree or a good grade. But that very same element of choice in personal writing can make it even more difficult for the blocked writer, since it requires much more internal discipline. (In fact, it could be said that the primary cause of blocking in personal writing is precisely that freedom of choice that is absent in other types of writing.)

Each of the four writing areas we discuss in Part 3 has

characteristic blocking causes. Business writers report that their problems tend to center on two major issues. First, managers need to know how to write in a way that is tactful and yet forceful, so that the job gets done or the problem solved, but the recipient of the letter or memo isn't offended. The objective is persuasion, getting employees to do what you want them to. The second typical business problem shows up when employees have to write for critical supervisors. Writing for an intimidating boss brings out the internal critic in full bloom, and the writer's struggle is intensified.

Student writers share the blocking problem of business workers. In the student world the critical reader is, of course, the teacher or the professor, instead of the boss. Students also face very explicit time pressures that exacerbate their blocking.

Technical/academic/professional writers block because they must try to remain objective about their material in order to convince other professionals that they are not intruding personal biases into their work. However, since language is a highly personal communication system, full of nuance and implication, this becomes extremely hard to do, especially for individuals who, as a group, tend to be unsophisticated and somewhat defensive about their command of language, compared with their competence with symbols, numbers, and charts.

You can use this section by turning to the chapter pertaining to your occupation or the kind of writing you most often do. But you may well find yourself simultaneously engaged in more than one type of writing—perhaps a memo, a resumé, and a thank-you note. So we recommend that you read through all of Part 3 at least once, carefully. Then feel free to pick and choose, to use your own discretion about how to mix and apply these techniques to *your* own special blocking problems.

In this section we set forth separate case histories of

blocking problems and their symptoms. Then we prescribe a set of treatment responses, drawn from the techniques in Part 2, one or two of which we develop fully in each case. We try to give examples that cover different stages of the writing process, as well as various kinds of writing products. We think you'll find the range of cases described and the treatments recommended extremely useful, whatever your particular situation.

7

Business Writing:

Letters, Memos, Proposals, Reports, Sales Brochures, Press Releases, Annual Reports

HAT happens when business writers block? Is there something characteristic about the business world and its special demands on writers that gives rise to blocking? In most business settings, the demanding pace and hectic environment are enough to cause hesitation and blocking—especially for anyone who has to concentrate on a slow, repetitive, introspective task like writing. In addition, business writers typically face the problem of establishing a constructive relationship with power. Since business organizations are hierarchical, a few people tell most of the others what to do. They wield power.

However, the business world is also one of complex interdependency. It's great to be part of the corporate team when everyone is meshing smoothly, sales are good, and you're all making money. But when one worker's inefficiency is holding everyone else back, and it's your job to solve that problem, things can get sticky fast.

The other end of the power relationship in business is fraught with its own blocking perils. Any employee has a powerful economic incentive to do what his bosses expect of him. But unlike bolting on car doors in an assembly line, writing isn't something you can force. So when you're under the gun in a business writing situation, there's always an edge of panic lurking just around the corner, waiting to spring out and engulf you if you waver. The pressure in these situations can become intolerable. And again, it readily leads to anger, fear, tension, and procrastination. Pressure tends to alert the internal critic, who then assumes the guise of the demanding supervisor. And unless it's crystal clear who will be reading the job and what they're like, audience confusion can also arise: How are you supposed to comfortably use a tone and style that a layman will find comprehensible without seeming to patronize your more knowledgeable supervisors? Conversely, how are you supposed to communicate a sophisticated corporate problem so that a member of the concerned public, for instance a shareholder, can understand what's going on and appreciate its genuine complexity? These are the problems that we cover in this chapter. We try to show you as graphically as possible how they can be resolved using the techniques presented and discussed in Part 2.

CASE 1: PROCRASTINATION

Often the goal of the writing task is a matter of managing or influencing someone else's behavior, and this fact can cause intense blocking in both the manager and the managed. Clearly this is a problem that transcends writing—it is a fundamental psychological issue in any complex human interraction—but in business writing it leads to specific blocking symptoms, especially procrastination. Here's an example of how Murray, the owner of a small textile company, found that his role as boss conflicted with his compassion for his staff to bring him slowly grinding to a halt in his writing.

> . . . so I find that the trickiest things to write are letters to my people where I've got to call them on the carpet for something. Say I've got a salesman and he's just not cutting it. He's in a slump. I've been waiting, watching, praying for months that he will snap out of it. But now I've got to step in and do something. I can't afford to wait around anymore. He's had plenty of warnings from me. Business is like that, you know. You wait around for things to get better and boom!—you're dead. Plus, I don't know what the guy's problem really is. Is his family falling apart? No, I don't think so . . . that I'd know about. So is he just off his feed? Who knows? But *my* neck is on the line here too. The guy may have been the greatest salesman in the world two years ago, but if he can't cut it now, I can't help it, he's not gonna last.
>
> So, I tell myself, okay, you got a job to do, Murray. First thing tomorrow, I'll come in and write that letter, first thing. I come in around 8:30, so I'll knock it out by 9:00. Well, tomorrow rolls around, the phone's ringing, two people in the office are out sick, we lose a shipment in Newark, and the letter's not getting written. You know? Then it's 10:00, 12:00, 5:00, and the letter's still not written. Something's always there to take my mind off it if I let it. That's what blocking is for me. I just don't want to come to grips with the problem, even if I know I have to.

Obviously, the problem is not simply that giving orders is hard to do. Managers and executives in all echelons of business do it every day, are used to doing it, and many enjoy doing it. The real blocking problem is that they get tense, feel angry, procrastinate, then get tenser and angrier, until they block completely. All because they worry about the most productive way to vent the irritation they feel. So they put it off . . . and off . . . and off. . . .

And when they do manage to sit down at a desk, they get impatient with the need to hit on just the right tone in the work. They don't want to be too harsh, nor too wishy-washy. The ideal is a forceful but not overly familiar or patronizing tone, one that is firm but not aggressive. It's the verbal equivalent of the iron hand in the velvet glove, and it requires the ability to balance writing diplomatically with subtle but unmistakable references to the big stick.

Blocking Symptoms: Murray's block is straightforward—he procrastinates. There's always something happening to distract him from his writing jobs, and since he's the boss, there's no one around who can force him to get the writing done. But even when he finally manages to get to his desk, Murray continues to block. He twists and fidgets, waiting for interruptions that will give him a legitimate excuse to avoid the frustrations of the unwritten page.

Prescription: CRANK LETTER, REVISER'S TOOL-KIT.   Murray's writing block stemmed from the emotional bind he was in: His anger at his salesman's declining effectiveness was conflicting with his concern for the person. It was clearly of the utmost importance that he try to communicate with his wayward employee, so that he could find out what the problem really was. He needed to warn the man gently but firmly that his poor performance was beginning to jeopardize his position with the company.

To do all this well, we suggested that Murray first vent his irritation in a Crank Letter so that he could then approach the writing task calmly and rationally. He gave our recommendation some careful thought, then drafted a letter along the lines we suggested. Here's how part of it sounded:

. . . Look, John, for Christ's sake, get off the stick—you're putting me and you in a hell of a spot and what's more you're keeping me completely in the dark about why you can't hack it anymore. And don't give me this crap about the territory drying up—I happen to know from Fedders that there's more new business coming out of the South than all the other regions combined. And why are you always out? Why can't I ever get in touch with you? Shape up, damnit!!

Once that was off his chest, Murray found he was able to relax and face the problem rationally. He was able to write a new draft that was just what he needed—cool, controlled, and collected, but to the point:

Dear John:

I know you must be under a lot of pressure, and I'm truly reluctant to add to it. However, you've missed your quota of new calls twice in the last three months and I'm deeply concerned about both you and the company's market position in your area. We cannot afford to let this kind of loss continue. We know that business is growing there—if we aren't selling, someone else must be.

Have a report on this week's calls on my desk by Monday noon. Otherwise we'll be forced to temporarily reduce both your draw and your base. Call to talk this action over with me if you need to, but remember, at this point it's up to you to produce.

We also found in our conversations with Murray that he felt gun-shy about dealing with written English. He felt that he'd never been very good at it, and although he was a superb and animated conversationalist, he wasn't comfortable with the basics of English grammar and style, and was very self-conscious about his poor spelling. Drawing from our Reviser's Toolkit, we soon convinced him that using a good dictionary and a basic style guide would quickly alleviate his insecurity in these areas and give him a much sharper sense of pleasure as his command over the mechanics of writing grew more certain.

CASE 2: PREWRITING OBSTACLES

Anthony C. works for an insurance company, writing up accident claim reports. Much of the work he does is relatively painless and routine: filling in blanks on forms, sending notification letters out to the insured claimants, and so on . . . no problem. But he sometimes has to write up brief summaries of a particular case for the company's legal department, and—*worst of all*—weekly reports on his progress on all the new work he's been assigned that week.

Blocking Symptoms: At these moments, Tony blocks. The light seems to become harsh and glaring. He yawns and stretches, and dully gazes around the office, seeing nothing in particular. He becomes acutely conscious of noises that he normally can tune out completely: the clicking of the typewriters, the ringing of the phones, footsteps, conversations, the murmur of the air conditioner. When people wander past his desk, his first impulse is to talk to them, but then he feels guilty because he has a job to do.

Prescription: MANAGING THE WRITING ENVIRONMENT, PULLING UP THE DRAWBRIDGE, MAKING WRITING APPOINTMENTS, GETTING TO KNOW THE INTERNAL CRITIC. Most of Tony's problems are prewriting obstacles. He needs to work on intentional preparation strategies when he knows he's going to be hit with one of the case writeups or progress reports that he tends to block on.

He may need to get out of the office altogether in order to manage his writing setting. Taking his files to the park, library, or even home for the weekend may give him the kind of absence of distraction that he needs in order to concentrate. Also, we said, he will find that fresh air and a short walk will help limber him up and relieve both his physical tension and his desire to procrastinate.

On the other hand, he may want to scout around and find a vacant office or conference room that isn't being used on Friday afternoons, then schedule his time so that he can make himself free to use this private space whenever he needs it. And when he does need it, he must actively segregate himself from the perverse temptations of the normal Friday afternoon slowdown in the office by Pulling Up the Drawbridge, closing the door, putting up a "Do Not Disturb" sign, having his calls held.

Finally, he needs to spend some time getting to know his internal critic, using the Portrayal and Dialogue with the Critic techniques we discuss in Part 2. The critic's insistent voice is giving him no trouble at all on his routine assignments, but it is becoming annoyingly intrusive when Tony has something more stressful to write than forms and notification letters.

CASE 3: CONFUSION OF PURPOSE

Working with Tony raised an interesting question in our minds: Was his blocking causing his supervisor, Charles A., any troubles? Were blocks showing up in his own writing? And if so, what was he doing about them? So we walked down the hall, knocked on his door, stepped in, and asked.

"No," he replied frankly. "Tony's problem isn't giving me any trouble. Even though his blocking makes writing into a very uncomfortable struggle for him, he *does* manage to meet his deadlines, or has so far anyway. However," Charles went on, "I do have a blocking problem of my own, a moderate one, caused by the consistent failure of branch offices to send me *their* weekly sales figures soon enough so that I can have them computed and analyzed for division meetings on Monday afternoons."

The company had just spent a small fortune on special electronic equipment designed to whisk information (including printed sheets) from branches to the home office via telephone, but all of this space-age gadgetry, said Charles, wasn't working worth a damn because the people at the other end weren't putting anything into it. He was trying to compose his third memo to them on the problem, and the need to put just the right amount of bite in his prose was making him block.

Blocking Symptoms: Unlike Tony, Charles had no trouble preparing to write. He was relaxed and confident, and had plenty to say. When we asked about getting a draft started, Charles instantly plucked up three or four sheets of paper from his desk, some with notes and scribbled lists, a few with abortive attempts at a rough draft.

At first we were inclined to think that Charles' block was at bottom a matter of suppressed anger. But the more we talked to him, the less likely this seemed. He had no trouble telling us how annoyed he felt at the reporting situation and stated repeatedly that he had been on the phone to every one of his branches innumerable times, begging, cajoling, demanding, and even shouting at the top of his lungs in order to make his point. They understood all too well, he said, how irritated he felt. But they needed to see it in writing, and so did his own superiors, who weren't pleased with the information logjam that was developing. Phone conversations were just too intangible, no matter how agitated and expressive he became. And a permanent record was needed for the files.

But when Charles tried to get it all down on paper, his head began to spin. "Dear Manager," he would write, add a few more lines, and then any one of a dozen possibilities came to mind. Should he start off with a reference to the electronic data transfer system, to computer schedules, to the need for programming lead time? Should he just jump right in and order deadline compliance, rather than worry about justifying his demand? Or should he describe, step-by-step, the best way for each branch to use the system to get the figures he needed to him on time? Every time he settled on a feasible approach, he simultaneously began to see the attractiveness of many others. His blocking, in short, was basically organizational.

Prescription: **WRITE A PURPOSE STATEMENT, PROFILE A (CRITICAL) READER, FRIENDLY EAR, PRE-EMPTING, SPOKE OUTLINES.** We started by suggesting Charles go back to basics. First, what was it he was trying to accomplish with this memo? What was the basic question it was intended to answer? He wrote his response: "To make sure that analyzed weekly sales figures can be reported in weekly division meetings." At first this sentence did not look especially helpful to him—it seemed too obvious and redundant. But as he sat staring at what he had written, Charles' eyes lit up and his brow began to unfurrow. "Wait a minute," he exclaimed, "I wonder if I have to have the information *analyzed* first. Maybe it can be reported in raw form at the Monday meeting, programmed afterward, and then redistributed in analyzed form the next day for comments."

He looked thoughtful and detached for a moment. We asked if he was wondering how the idea would go over with his superiors and the other division chiefs. He nodded. "Try to Profile a (Critical) Reader, a quick one, right now, off the top of your head, before you even try to write the memo again," we urged him. "Do it orally, with the two of us acting as a quartet of Friendly Ears, to save you time." He sat back, laced his fingers across his stomach, gazed up at the ceiling, and talked steadily for the next thirty minutes.

We didn't even have to suggest Pre-empting—he was already anticipating possible objections to his plan and skillfully rebutting them. At the end of the hour, we rose, added a comment about the value of Spoke Outlines, and left him scribbling furiously away on a fresh sheet of paper.

CASE 4: OVERLAPPING PROJECTS

Stacey C. is a community affairs specialist for an international drug company. "I face constant, hourly, intense pressure to produce a wide range of written documents," she told us. Her most recent episode of blocking had come about like this:

> Next week I'm meeting with a community group that is extremely upset with our plans to acquire a number of old residential hotels in a low-income neighborhood in their area. We want to tear them down to build a new manufacturing plant.
>
> I'm on the spot on this one. I've got to justify the company's actions to a volatile and politically savvy bunch of residents. Fortunately, I've got a good argument to make to them: jobs. The problem is that they've asked to see our development proposal for the area, including our plans for re-housing residents in these units and the exact percent of jobs that will go to neighborhood residents, and I've got to pull that information together out of a half-dozen different sources. It has to be put into clear, comprehensible language too, because if there's one item or paragraph in the proposal that sounds vague, bureaucratic, or fishy to them, they'll rip me to shreds. In addition, I've got to make the proposal work for my supervisor, since it has to reflect

our genuine intentions, of course, and he wants to keep tabs on my work.

Now, all that's just one of a half-dozen things I've got to do before Friday, and each one means putting something on paper. It's driving me nuts. There are times when I think I'm either going crazy or having a heart attack. I get dizzy, my breath gets short, my knees get weak, and I feel faint and nauseous. If this were the nineteenth century, I'd describe it as "swooning."

Blocking Symptoms: If you're in a position like Stacey's, you know that business writing is deadline writing — you feel you never have enough time to do the job right. Because your deadlines are always unrealistically short, you're stuck in a perennial game of catch-up, always trying to tie up the leftover loose ends on the last job when you should be laying the groundwork for the next one.

It's the mental equivalent of being on a treadmill that won't ever slow down enough so that you can catch your breath. Inevitably there come moments when your mind rebels and you come to a screeching psychological halt — you block, desperate for a little slack in your jammed agenda. You look at the page and find that your overloaded brain is short-circuiting: You can't even read what you've just written, let alone move on to the next line and try to create something new. All you really want to do is crawl off and go to sleep somewhere.

Prescription: CREATIVE JUGGLING, SYSTEMATIC RELAXATION STRATEGIES, FOG INDEX, DICK-AND-JANING. We found Stacey was already an accomplished scheduler. Working backward from deadline dates to determine daily quotas for a job was old hat to her. She knew approximately how long each job was likely to take, and she was shrewd enough to add on a margin of safety for slippage and the unforeseen contingencies that always eat up your writing time. She was a past master at making writing appointments with herself and sticking to them. She had no trouble insisting on privacy when she needed it.

But oddly enough, she hadn't developed the ability to leave one project in the middle, when she was momentarily blocked, and jump to the next one for a while. Instead, she had the fixed notion that each job had to be doggedly followed from beginning to end until it was finished. Then and only then could she let herself move on to the next one.

That, we suggested, was the heart of her blocking problem. We discussed it with her, and concluded that she might not get so anxious if she could teach herself to work on all her jobs for the week concurrently, rather than stringing them out like beads on a string. The way she was doing it now, we said, the pressure to get to work on projects she'd postponed until later in the week was building up to intolerable levels, making her concerned and panicky, distracting her from the job at hand, wasting her time, and making her block.

Stacey listened to us and grimaced. "But I can't let go of something I'm in the middle of," she complained. "I just can't bring myself to step away from it—it makes me too tense to do that." So try a Systematic Relaxation method, like PMR, we replied. It took some convincing to get her to make time in her schedule for serious relaxation exercise, but she eventually followed our advice. Now she tells us that she's been able to nearly double her productivity, just by relaxing.

Finally, we touched on a specific problem confronting Stacey with this particular proposal: How to reduce a lot of corporate and legal abstractions about the forthcoming project into simple, plain, accurate English. We went over rewriting techniques, especially the Fog Index, but also Dick-and-Janing. When she got lost in a terminological fog, we said, she could reduce it all to one-syllable, five- or six-word sentences, like this:

Abex wants to build a plant. It wants to do so soon. The

plant will be in Southside. There is a problem. Houses will be torn down. But there is a bonus, too. The new plant will hire people . . .

CASE 5: THE PERFECTIONIST KNIFE

Clayton K. is one of three partners in a small public relations firm that handles promotion for a number of rock groups. Among many other things, he writes all the press releases the company puts out, and does them well. He has the right tone of terse intimacy down cold. Clients love his copy. Attendance soars. His writing magic works.

But he's written at least a hundred of these releases in the last three months, and he's beginning to run dry.

Blocking Symptoms: Success itself is paralyzing Clayton. The relentless demand to turn in another award-winning performance is making him freeze up. The old saying, "You're only as good as your last performance," has taken on a chilling ring.

Now when he sits down to write, his hands get cold and clammy, and his head starts to throb. Irrelevant jingles and themes from his kids' TV shows run obsessively through his mind. He's noticing a perverse tendency in himself to want to write the next release as a joke, to twist it into satire. What worries him, of course, is that he hasn't been able to keep on steadily turning them out.

Prescription: PAST-SUCCESS SPRINGBOARD, TREA-SURY, FRIENDLY EAR. Our advice to Clayton was simple: If you have to drive yourself compulsively, at least try to do it with compassion. Use the Past-Success Springboard to remind yourself that you already have some solid achievements to your credit. You're definitely not starting from scratch. Sit down in your office, put your feet up, pull some past triumphs out of your files, blow the dust off them, and let your memory linger on how good you felt about them. Tell yourself it's not a question of *whether* you will succeed; you've always come through in the past. However difficult it was, you've done it before. There's no reason to believe you can't do it again.

One reason Clayton's having trouble with this particular writing task is that he's bored. His job has lost its challenge. He's worked on this kind of project so many times that there are no surprises in it anymore.

This, we told him, is precisely why professional writers keep Treasury files, for just this kind of emergency. If Clayton had been collecting creative and insightful verbal trinkets, now would be the time to pull them out and sift through them.

At best, and our writing friends agree with us that this happens surprisingly often, he would find a phrase, a word, an idea—something that would jog his mind into new paths and help open it up to a fresh approach. At worst, and this is by no means a trivial result, he would have given himself an invigorating mental recess from the frustration of trying to work when his head felt like it was full of moths.

Finally, we urged Clayton to develop a Friendly Ear— someone to talk to who is interested yet impartial, who can listen calmly and compassionately when he's under pressure and his fears of incipient failure begin to mount and make him block. A Friendly Ear could give him valuable moral support, as well as thoughtful feedback on how his compositional ideas sound.

The kind of blocking that Clayton suffers from results from what poet Louise Bogan calls "the knife of the perfectionist attitude in art and life." He feels a blade at his throat, ready to drain his lifeblood away if he falters. Pressure like this can literally be fatal. It causes heart disease in many aggressive, hard-driving people. Clayton should give himself a break, to slow down, relax, and look around.

CASE 6: THE AMBIGUOUS AUDIENCE

Joan G. has been preparing sales brochures for a small California electronics firm for a couple of years now, and both she and her supervisors feel that the experience of writing for buyers as well as sales reps has adequately prepared her to take on the job of writing the company's annual report this year. But now she's not so sure. The report will be read by colleagues, other employees, management, shareholders, and the general public. Joan can't quite figure out how to slant it so that it will appeal to everyone. She doesn't want to insult the intelligence of corporate insiders, but she also doesn't want to mystify the lay reader.

Blocking Symptoms: Joan's blocking isn't severe enough to keep her from writing, but the job is taking too long because she just can't quite hit on the right tone. She's written draft after draft, but each one sounds either too flat or too abstract to her. More than anything else, she's feeling detached from the job, as though she were in a slight mental fog all the time. And the deadline, which cannot be postponed, is looming larger and larger in the now not-so-distant future.

One of the trickiest problems in business writing arises when you have to pull together something that will be read by widely different audiences. This situation commonly crops up in the production of annual reports, which are read by stockbrokers, job seekers, board members, employees, auditors, and shareholders, to name only a few types of readers. Annual reports serve a multitude of functions for a wide spectrum of readers, and trying to respond to their divergent curiosities can make even the most seasoned writer block.

Prescription: PROFILE A (CRITICAL) READER, READ IT OUT LOUD, THE ARCHIVES BOX.   When we read over Joan's drafts, we soon realized that the answer to her problem was a simple one: She just didn't have a sufficiently concrete and vivid sense of a typical reader. "Yes," she agreed, "but how can you talk about a 'typical' reader? There are so many different kinds of readers for this report, each with a different point of view, that I don't quite see how having a sharper sense of their interests and expectations would help me."

True, we conceded, but what that implied to us was that all she needed to do was sample both ends of the spectrum. If she could write to the least common denominator—an intelligent, interested, but uninformed member of the public—and then also make the text work for a completely knowledgeable insider, she would have the audience bracketed, and her fogginess would clear up.

We suggested this approach: Treat us as though we were a living, composite profile of the typical reader, and read your latest draft out loud to us. She did, and we stopped her when we needed clarification, or felt the text rambled on too long or missed the point. Gradually Joan became more and more enthusiastic about the exercise.

When she had finished, we then went on to recommend that now that she had a fairly clear idea of how a lay reader would respond to the work, she should take that same draft and do the same thing with a reader who represented the other end of the spectrum—an informed, sophisticated, interested insider, like one of her supervisors. Read it out loud, we said, while he or she listens and gives critical feedback. Not only will this clarify that particular type of reader's expectations, it should also open up a dialogue with those Joan needs to please—her bosses—and constructively involve them in the process of getting the report completed, on time, the way they want it done. It was also, we pointed out, a subtle way to elicit their tacit approval of the work while it is still in progress.

Because we thought we detected a slight reluctance on Joan's part to give up any of the material she had so laboriously produced for previous drafts, we mentioned the Archives Box technique, which would permit her to keep in reserve and resurrect at will anything she cut while revising. This advice helped her make drastic, but necessary, cuts.

8

Student Writing:

Essay Exams, Themes, and Research Papers

HE internal critic is modeled on the admonitions and warnings that we receive when very young, first from parents, then from teachers and other authority figures, and finally from employers. In student writings the teacher is the critic incarnate. School is where we first learn the rules, which of course have the effect of defining precisely what we fear we won't be able to measure up to. As a consequence, it's easy to see why writing assignments in school easily elicit blocking.

In this chapter we offer you examples of how students have been able to use these techniques to work through their blocks. We also urge you to revise your attitudes about your instructors. A good teacher, who is doing the job properly, should be willing to act as your Friendly Ear, not just your external critic. We recommend that you accept your teacher as an ally, one who will listen dispassionately and sympathetically while you explore your thoughts on the topic, then gently guide you in the most promising directions. You will rarely find any other writing situation in which all four functions of critic, Friendly Ear, audience, and teacher appear in one accessible person—so take advantage of it!

The overall function of student writing at all levels—from the elementary grades through graduate school—is to demonstrate the student's command over a given body of ideas and information, to show the ability to absorb, understand, organize, and express a coherent sequence of thoughts in writing.

In addition to the stranglehold exerted by the critic, there are three special types of demands in student writing that lead to unique kinds of blocking. First, there are timed essay exams, calculated to test your mastery of a subject and designed to make you work quickly. The blocking that occurs during these exams almost always results from either letting tension get the upper hand or from failing to prepare adequately by researching the subject area thoroughly.

The second type of student writing is the theme, usually developed over a period of a few days or a week, and intended to evaluate the ability to present a personal but reasoned argument expressing the student's opinion on a given topic. Because theme writing usually means that you have to express an opinion on a subject that you had little prior understanding of, you fear that your paper will seem banal, unoriginal, incomplete, and inaccurate. You stumble over how to get into the topic, how much supporting information to include, and how to persuade a critical reader of your point of view. This type of assignment can evoke blocking across all four stages of the writing process.

The third type of student writing task is the research paper. This category consists of the longest papers a student may ever have to write, including theses and dissertations. Again, the blocking that can occur spans the entire writing process, but it tends to be concentrated in two areas: information collecting and organization. The problem with the first is, as often as not, an overabundance rather than a lack of data. If you feel swamped by data, you may freeze up. And the organization problem may occur whenever one deals with voluminous amounts of data over an extended period of time.

Students who major in the humanities have an easier time with the fundamentals of the writing process than those whose majors, such as math and business administration, place more emphasis on numbers than on words. Students who regard themselves primarily as "numerate" rather than "literate" may want to look over our discussion of technical writing in Chapter 9.

Blocking affects every student, at some time, at some stage of the writing process. So if you're having a tough time of it, don't despair. You're not alone. Others, many others, have met and mastered these same obstacles. Read on, and you'll see more clearly how they did it.

CASE 1: FEAR OF WRITING

Randy N. is a senior in Business Administration at the University of California, Berkeley. Over the four years of his undergraduate work, he's had to compose an occasional paper, but most of his classes haven't required much writing from him. And when he *has* had to write, he's only managed to turn in a barely acceptable draft, and the process of pulling it together has always been a struggle. Now, however, Randy has a problem. In order to graduate, he has to pass two quarters of a basic composition class, one in which a weekly theme is required. Having postponed the class for four years, he now has to face it. Unfortunately, he's built up so much dread about it that he's blocking badly about even attending the class.

Blocking Symptoms: If you are like Randy, you feel panicky and resentful when you have to write. Even the very thought of it depresses you. The classroom, the books you have to read, and especially the teacher all intimidate you. You're afraid to write because you're convinced you can't say anything clearly—much less persuasively or interestingly. When you actually try to compose something, your chest tightens up and your palms get sweaty. You're easily distracted. Deadlines creep closer and closer and yet you make no progress.

Prescription: MANAGE YOUR WRITING ENVIRONMENT: USING PROPS, PULLING UP THE DRAWBRIDGE, GETTING TO KNOW THE INTERNAL CRITIC, A FRIENDLY EAR, BRAINSTORMING, SCHEDULE CRITICAL INPUT FROM OTHERS, PREEMPTING, CHANGE THE MEDIUM. Randy was his own worst enemy. He exaggerated verbal ineptness to the point that he was becoming virtually phobic about anything connected with the writing class, the teacher, and for that matter the entire English department.

We began by describing to him the value of actively Managing his Writing Environment. Writing goes more smoothly, we said, when one's surroundings reflect the point of the activity there. Even the position of the desk, chair, rug, and other furnishings act as symbols (and reminders) of the writing task. By starting with a completely familiar and secure setting, such as a room in his apartment, and rearranging it for the express purpose of writing, Randy could begin to break down his conditioned hypersensitivity to the writing process. We also mentioned the value of Props (later we learned that an old sweatshirt worked for Randy), as well as the necessity of learning to secure his privacy when he needed it.

But the heart of our recommendation to Randy was to Get to Know His Internal Critic. When the concept of the internal critic and its development had been explained, he agreed that it made some sense. He was somewhat reluctant at first to believe that mere Portrayals and Dialogues with the

Critic would have much influence on his blocking, which had acquired a rocklike solidity in his mind, but he agreed to try them anyway. He later reported to us, with noticeable relief, that they had decreased the intensity of his block. In fact, though he was still somewhat anxious, he had begun to feel amused about his former terror. After all, he knew perfectly well that the concepts and words were in his head somewhere, and that it was really his own fantasies that had bullied him into this paralysis.

From that point on, the remainder of our prescription for Randy boiled down to two things: Get to know your teacher better so that you can understand and adopt some of your teacher's critical skills, and work on developing certain revision skills. Specifically, we suggested that Randy combine Pre-empting and Scheduling Critical Input from his teacher with developing the teacher as a Friendly Ear. In effect, he should make the teacher into a friendly critic. If he wanted to start at a less intimidating level, he could begin by talking his ideas and drafts over with other students. When he had trouble coming up with a good approach to the weekly topic, we added, he might want to form a Brainstorming group. He could enlist his teacher's assistance after he felt comfortable about exposing his thinking processes to someone else.

When he had finished a draft of a paper, he should then make an appointment for the professor's office hours, so that he was actively taking charge of the process of receiving critical feedback. Before meeting with the professor, he could go back over the draft and examine it closely for logical or grammatical flaws, in effect using the Pre-empting technique. We also suggested that he set the entire draft aside for a day or two, time permitting, before rereading it with a fresher, more objective eye, and that he get it into typed form as soon as possible so that he could get accustomed to the visual changes that transforming longhand into typescript produces.

We concluded our conversations with Randy by pointing out that most teachers, particularly teachers of English classes, welcome close personal interaction with their students, since it provides an opportunity to look over an actual sample of the student's work, which is hard to do in a large class. Build as rich an interaction as possible, we said, and after you get your paper back, make another appointment to discuss the critical comments with your professor.

CASE 2: TOO MUCH INFORMATION

A few months ago, Cheryl W. dragged herself into Karin's office and wearily dropped a stack of notes the size of a telephone book onto Karin's desk. She was working on a lengthy research paper about the Protestant Reformation for a history seminar, and she had stopped by Karin's office for a short respite from her toils in the library. Aware that Cheryl's paper was due in less than a month, Karin wondered aloud why she was still researching. Cheryl replied that she had tried to start a draft numerous times without success and felt that her only choice was to keep on developing more familiarity with her subject, in hopes that a suitable organizing framework would appear along the way.

Blocking Symptoms: Cheryl feels smothered by the sheer quantity of information she has accumulated on her topic. After months of research work, she has accumulated masses of material, most of which is directly pertinent to her subject, some of which is indirectly related but interesting. Cheryl has a fairly clear idea of what her central purpose is, but she can't seem to get the material structured so that it makes sense and fits each part into a logical place in the conceptual flow of the work. She has been retreating to the safe world of reading and note-taking, rather than forging ahead to the next stage of the process. And furthermore, when she tries to start a rough draft, she seems to parrot her notes instead of writing in her own words. She feels hopelessly unoriginal. She's anxious, frustrated, dissatisfied, and above all, stuck.

Prescription: **FRIENDLY EAR, WRITE A PURPOSE STATEMENT, LISTS, OUTLINING, SPOKE OUTLINES, COOKER SHEETS.** Karin's conversation with Cheryl that day went on for some time, with Karin automatically adopting the role of Friendly Ear. The conversation started like this:

KARIN: Tell me briefly what you've learned.

CHERYL: I've learned more about abuses in the sixteenth century Catholic Church than I ever wanted to know. I've learned about the rising middle class, secular values, and growing nationalism, all centrifugal forces pulling people away from the church. It's a wonder that any part of Europe remained Catholic at all.

KARIN: I wonder why some countries remained in the fold and others didn't?

CHERYL: I think the outcome depended as much on purely political considerations as it did on religious issues. Compare England and Germany, for instance. If Henry VIII's first wife had borne a son, he wouldn't have sued for divorce and set his country on a path leading away from the church. If Germany had had a unified central government, it wouldn't have fallen prey to so many abuses and taxes, which fanned discontent with Rome. When Luther's movement spread, the squabbling among the small states in Germany over political concerns was often as important as purely religious arguments.

KARIN: So what you're saying is that politics was just as important as religion in determining the course of the Reformation.

CHERYL: Yes. I know enough about the political questions to develop that argument. I'll contrast the political conditions in two countries to show why Reformation took the course it did. I'm ready and eager to write, but my problem is how to organize the argument.

Continuing in her role as Friendly Ear, Karin's first question was whether Cheryl had written out a Purpose Statement. She hadn't, so Karin mentioned the advantages of orienting one's organizational thinking around an overall goal, stated in clear, simple terms and referred back to repeatedly, so that all of the writing related to it in some well-defined way.

She also suggested that Cheryl immediately begin the process of transmuting her thick stack of 3 x 5 index cards into *Lists*, as a way of condensing her material enough so that she could see more clearly where she stood.

The rest of Karin's conversation with Cheryl was a detailed discussion of the organizational strategies that we have provided for you in Part 2, including Profiling a Critical Reader and Outlines, especially Spoke Outlines.

Since Cheryl had complained that she often felt as though she were simply repeating what her research sources had said, and that she really hadn't made the information her own, Karin's final comment involved the use of Cooker Sheets as a way of developing her own perspectives on the topic and refining her understanding of the issues.

In research blocking, Cooker Sheets also serve an important specialized function: They help bring the information-gathering stage to a close, help you know when to stop researching, by showing you when you have enough support for your own point of view.

CASE 3: FAILURE TO MANAGE TIME

Sitting in the room where her final exam in Political Science is being given, Christine L. feels a familiar panic welling up in her. She fights it, but it's too strong. Her stomach churns and her breathing becomes rapid and shallow. The pen feels slick with sweat, and her exam book sticks to her damp palms. She's worked all night reviewing the class texts and her notes, but now her mind feels uncomfortably cluttered with miscellaneous, incoherent scraps and fragments. As the minutes pass by, her anxiety grows stronger and her responses to the questions grow more and more superficial and clichéd.

Blocking Symptoms: Christine gets too tense to formulate adequate responses on timed essay exams. Writing under pressure robs her of her powers of concentration. Fatigued and jumpy, she draws a blank on material she thought she knew backward and forward.

Prescriptions: MAKE WRITING APPOINTMENTS, CREATIVE JUGGLING, SYSTEMATIC RELAXATION TECHNIQUES, LISTS, FROSTING FIRST, PAST-SUCCESS SPRINGBOARD, DICK-AND-JANING. Christine's fundamental blocking problems stemmed, we found, from her failure to manage her preparation time well. "How can I finish this History paper, get ready for my next final, which is in Chemistry, and write up the weekly theme for my Sociology class, all in three days?" lamented Christine to us the day after her ordeal at the Political Science exam.

Well, we responded, you can manage your time by making firm plans to write at certain hours of the day, then adhering to your schedule doggedly, no matter what kind of temptations, demands, and distractions come your way. Also, we added, you should try Creative Juggling. It's easier to begin and complete a writing project if you know that when you tire of it, you can set it aside temporarily and jump to another one. Don't make the common, compulsive mistake of thinking that you have to finish one project before going on to the next.

Managing your time well should reduce tension and stress. Some tension under test conditions is normal and useful because it helps you concentrate and speeds up your thought processes. But too much tension can paralyze you. You will want to learn and regularly practice a Systematic Relaxation technique, we added.

If you're worried that relaxing your body will dull your mental capacities, try this test. The next time you're writing at home, interrupt yourself at some point and deliberately relax your muscles. Then go back to work and notice the effect this brief pause has had on your mental processes. Usually our students report that they find new, creative thoughts coming to them, and fresh powers of analysis and description appear.

If you're particularly susceptible to physical tension during exams, you may also find it useful to rehearse on the exam, either alone or with a group of other students. Compose a set of sample questions, set a time limit corresponding to that of the real exam, and write out your answers fully. Even if you can't use your rehearsal answers under the real test conditions, the experience of sitting comfortably through a testlike situation while answering tough questions will give you a feeling of mastery that will carry over into the actual test setting.

In fact, you can even rehearse in your mind. Psychologists, who call this technique "behavioral rehearsal," have documented its benefits. Make the mental scene vivid and detailed and visualize yourself staying absolutely relaxed throughout the entire exam. You can even stop, back up, and mentally repeat over and over any parts of the experience that make you tense. When you're completely relaxed, move ahead again.

We finally outlined for Christine several techniques to use during the exam itself, so that she could get the first words down on paper. When you read the questions, we said, many points that you want to make in your answers will flash through your mind. Get them down on paper in a List. Then pick the topic that feels easiest to you—go for the Frosting First. There's no need to start with question 1 and work through to question 10, taking each one in sequence. No one will care which you answered first as long as you do them all. Also, getting the easiest ones out of the way as fast as possible is an efficient way to use time because it frees as much of the exam period as possible for working on the tougher questions.

Once you're into the test, if you feel your word stream drying up, try two continuation techniques: Dick-and-Janing and the Past Success Springboard. Using the first of these to transform your List into a series of one-syllable, five-word sentences will provide a valuable intermediate step between your random notes and the smooth narrative.

And finally, give yourself an occasional morale booster by reminding yourself of specific occasions in the past when you've taken a demanding exam and come through it triumphantly. Having done it before, you know you can do it again.

9

Technical, Academic, and Professional Writing

Grant Proposals, Research Reports, Professional Journal and Popular Magazine Articles, Team-Written Reports

W HEN professionals in scientific or intellectual fields need to write, they may experience all the blocks that are encountered in any other area of writing. But technical/academic/professional writers are particularly susceptible to certain specific types of blocking, including self-doubt about ability to use language effectively.

With the exception of professional technical writers and some academic researchers, primarily those in the humanities, most technical, scientific, and academic writers do not feel confident about their command of the mechanics of language, and they do not enjoy writing. This conflict seems to be an occupational hazard of the scientific and technical professions. Because of the emphasis on the quantitative in their training, members of professions like engineering, medicine, accounting, economics—in short, most of the pure and applied sciences—are often bewildered and at a loss when dealing with the nuances and ambiguities of language. It seems elusive and slippery to them, particularly to those whose lifelong affinity is for numbers, symbols, and diagrams, rather than words. (Thanks to Shirley Hentzell, a veteran technical editor, we've come to refer to these individuals as "numerate" rather than "literate.")

For these numerates, unblocking may require some remedial study of Prose Mechanics, to familiarize themselves with the basic rules of grammar and the mechanical details of spelling and punctuation. Our bibliography includes an excellent work on English grammar by George O. Curme, which we recommend for this purpose. Numerates usually benefit from reading in areas outside their specialties. Reading good fiction is a painless way to refresh your sense of the infinite number of elegant ways to put words together.

Another common blocking problem in technical/academic/professional writing is caused by the attempt to write as "objectively" as possible, that is, to produce a thorough, sober, and logical presentation of the facts, with as little personal bias or emotional coloring as possible. This may sound simple, but it's not. Because the purpose of professional/technical/academic writing is to allow the reader to draw his or her own conclusions from the information given, the problem arises in trying to keep your own personal perspectives as far in the background of the text as possible.

Ideally, you try to make your prose function like a pane of glass, through which the reader can see your methodology, data, analyses, and results with as little as possible of your own personal interpretation of them. This is no small task. Striving to remain as detached as possible when writing about a subject that you know well, have studied for years, and have passionate feelings about is a natural cause of blocking. You've done the research, collected the data, conducted the experiments, and now you want to report the results as accurately as possible. You want your reader to see the outcome the way you believe it should be seen. But you also want the reader to agree with you by drawing conclusions independently. In short, you want to be accurate, but you also want to be right, and you want others to agree that you're right. So, caught between your strong desire to persuade and an equally strong allegiance to scientific or intellectual precision, you freeze up.

A third common problem in academic/technical/ professional writing is the sheer sophistication of the subject matter. By definition, if you're involved in "research" you're developing concepts that are new and complex. You're at the frontiers of knowledge, and what you're doing there involves discovering and exploring new ways of seeing and understanding a problem or topic.

The reality of this sophistication raises two further issues that relate closely to blocking. First, because your subject is usually highly specialized and you've undergone years of mental preparation to understand it yourself, you know just how complicated it really is, and you want to do justice to every one of its many aspects. Since you see the significance of every detail, you resist placing them in a hierarchical sequence, where some facts take on more prominence than others. This is organizational blocking. What should be subordinate to what becomes an issue. You struggle to create a narrative framework that will give each fact or subtopic its appropriate attention and weight. Because doing all this takes patience and concentration, it can easily bring on fatigue, resistance, and writing paralysis.

In addition, working with highly sophisticated information can bring on blocking when you have to explain it—in effect *translate* it—for a lay audience. Conflict results when you want readers to understand your work, but you don't want to oversimplify your subject.

For example, a public health physician may have concluded a study that implicates a common household substance as a potential carcinogen; or an engineer may have invented a new way to pour and prestress concrete so that massive structures can be erected using less reinforcing steel and less cement. And they both want to make their findings available to the public. But conflict and confusion arise in trying to write this type of communication because the physician and engineer can't be sure how much their readers know about the field. Do their terms, procedures, and underlying premises need to be explained fully, or will readers be familiar with some of this information? Many technical/academic/professionals work in isolation in order to concentrate, and they tend to lose touch with the attitudes and expectations that the lay reader will bring to their writing.

Finally, blocking in technical/academic/professional writing also stems from the need to assert your credibility. If you claim to advance the sum of human knowledge, your work will be closely examined by others—lay readers and professional peers alike—for originality and validity. While you want to be dispassionate and unbiased, you also want to let your reader know that you are an expert, one who knows the field and deserves to be heard. But asserting that claim can be highly intimidating if you fear the scrutiny by other experts, or doubt that you have the right to make the claim in the first place. You block. And when you do try to write, you hedge your prose with so many qualifiers—*in our opinion, may, might, could, it seems, perhaps, tends to*, and so on—that the heart of the message is completely obscured . . . all that comes through is your doubt and hesitation.

For the blocked technical/academic/professional worker, writing can seem like a mysterious, tortured, insurmountable chore. Given the desire to overcome it, however, blocking in this type of writing is highly amenable to the influence of the techniques presented below. As you have probably already discovered, rarely can any professional escape the need to write. But bear in mind that you do not have to become a master wordsmith in order to become a competent and effective writer. Unblocking and learning to compose smoothly are more than anything else a function of basic qualities—such as hard work and discipline—that preparing for your profession has already made you familiar with, and which you can readily bring to bear on the problem of blocking and the practice of writing.

CASE 1: LANGUAGE PRACTICE

Alan J. is a troubleshooter for Transitron, a small, dynamic, prestigious computer firm. When a company that uses their equipment hits a glitch, they call Alan. Usually he can handle it over the phone, but sometimes a memo, a brief letter, or even a short report is called for, and that's where Alan's personal troubleshooting skills lapse.

Blocking Symptoms: When Alan sits down to write, all he can think of are trite, hackneyed expressions. The same dull phrases run through his mind over and over, like the proverbial broken record. None of the words he digs up seem to accurately label the concept or procedure that he wants to describe. He knows what he wants to say, but he doesn't seem to be able to say it without spending hours and hours with his thesaurus, dictionary, and typewriter.

As a result, he tends to push his writing chores to the back of his mind—and his desk—and they don't get done on time. He wonders resentfully why he can't just stick to his calculator, computer, blackboard, and the mathematical tools that he's so used to.

Prescription: KEEPING A WRITER'S LOG, GETTING TO KNOW THE INTERNAL CRITIC, and REVISER'S TOOLKIT. Blocking in Alan's case stemmed from two things: insufficient practice with the range and scope of language, and the presence of a specialized version of the internal critic. Alan's critic felt comfortable when he was exercising his quantitative skills but became anxious and suppressive when he tried to venture into verbal waters.

Consequently, we first recommended Keeping a Writer's Log, and we described the technique, touching on the nature of the free-associative approach to it and the value of writing in it at regular times. Keeping a log, we told him, gives a blocked writer a secure linguistic arena in which to begin to exercise and expand his or her verbal skills without the risk of exposing them to the scrutiny of the outside world.

Write about your frustrated feelings about writing, we said. Use that irritation and resentfulness as a potentially rich starting point. Get it down on the page, and see where it leads you. Becoming self-absorbed in a log will open up the resources of your unconscious and animate your thinking about language, while it actually engages you in exercising and developing your writing skills. Alan agreed to try the logging method.

We then set forth the concept of the internal critic and told Alan how we thought his own internal critic was contributing to his block. Alan responded that he thought of the critic as more of a wary spectator than an active decision-making influence on his moods and attitudes. Well, get to know him and find out for sure, we replied, and we described the Portrayal and Dialoguing methods.

Finally we recommended some basic, practical ways for Alan to broaden his understanding of English, including the continued use of a good thesaurus and a good dictionary. We offered him a list of reference works and urged him to read more, especially well-written popular journals and popular fiction. It doesn't have to be fine literature, we said, just good, well-written prose, something that will open up the possibilities that English has to offer—and entertain you at the same time.

CASE 2: WRITING FOR NONSPECIALISTS

A biologist, Frederick A., had developed a process for cultivating protein-rich algae that could be easily converted into an abundant and extremely inexpensive food source. Frederick had all the theoretical data he needed to convince other scientists in his field that the process was feasible, but he needed to set up and evaluate a demonstration experiment, one that would apply the theoretical model to a real-life test.

To conduct his experiment, he needed a grant, and he knew that that meant submitting proposals to the National Science Foundation, the National Institutes of Health, the Department of Agriculture, the Ford Foundation, and some of the other large private grantmakers. In order to convince these potential funders that he deserved their support, Frederick had to somehow translate his stacks of diagrams, designs, charts, and page after page of mathematical formulas into a clear, crisp, well-structured proposal narrative. But the prospect of having to do all this in plain English left him feeling blocked and hopeless. "How," he asked us, "can I possibly give a persuasive account of this work if I have to simplify it so much that I'm not representing the ideas fully and accurately?"

Blocking Symptoms: Knowing his work is going to be read by a lay audience is making Frederick block. On the one hand, he feels that the research must speak for itself. How can he simplify it without losing its detail, comprehensiveness, and accuracy? On the other hand, he suspects that his colleagues will look down their noses at his work if he has "watered it down" for public consumption.

Prescription: FRIENDLY EAR, PROFILE OF A (CRITICAL) READER, SENSORY MONOLOGUE, NONSTOPS, AND DICK-AND-JANING. Frederick was blocking because he was uncomfortable with plain, straightforward exposition, and secretly afraid that his colleagues would sneer at anything written in popular, nontechnical terms.

His problem highlights the crucial importance of knowing your audience. In Frederick's case, Karin helped him begin to unblock and understand his typical reader more vividly by assuming that role herself and getting him to explain to her in conversational terms just what he was trying to accomplish.

> It's really very simple. I have developed a process for cultivating a protein-rich alga suitable for human consumption. I've done the work in my laboratory, but you could do it in a swimming pool, and a nomad tribesman could do it in a stagnant pond. All you need is a sample to seed the water, a few chemicals to initiate the process, and then you wait.
>
> After a few weeks, the alga adheres to the bottom of the pond and can be scraped off. It looks like a piece of green plastic, it's chewy (but not particularly tasty, I'm afraid), and it's richer in protein than soybeans. I have some samples right here . . . want to try one?
>
> It lasts indefinitely and requires only stagnant water and sunlight to reproduce. It's a food source that can feed people who are starving right now, a process that requires no high technology, and I'm convinced that it will be a terrific success, if only I can get the funds to run a rigorous demonstration project.

At about this point, Karin interrupted Frederick and

told him that he was dictating the rough draft of the introduction to the proposal and that he should Tape It. Talking to a flesh-and-blood embodiment of a typical reader, someone unfamiliar with his field, had helped Frederick to focus and clarify his thoughts and thus to find the best way to explain his work to a lay reader.

Karin's next suggestion was that Frederick try using Sensory Monologues and then Nonstops to keep the words flowing once he started writing. Later he reported that these techniques had worked well. He had used the numerous illustrations and charts in his files as points of departure. Each figure had triggered a fresh chain of description and conceptualization, and had produced a new page or two of very rough draft. Also, using a dictaphone for the rough draft, pretending that he was still talking to Karin, and then having a transcript typed up later was an easier way for him to compose than by actually sitting down with pen and paper.

Karin finally suggested to Frederick that if his abstract technical prose style returned and the work became unnecessarily verbose and disorganized, he could always find his way back to the basic thread of the story by reducing it to the short, simple sentences of Dick-and-Janing.

CASE 3: TEAM WRITING

Peter J., an aeronautical engineer, was managing his first team-written, multi-million dollar proposal for his company. His role was to receive and coordinate draft sections from other researchers, then write up the abstract, introduction, and background sections. Some members of his team he knew well, but others were total strangers to him.

He assigned everyone separate sections of the draft to write up, then sat back to wait. But that's where problems arose. He found that there was more interdependence among the various sections than he had expected: Contributors felt that they couldn't really go ahead with their separate parts until they knew what the overall narrative structure was like and could see how to relate their sections to the larger whole. Peter, on the other hand, felt that he couldn't go ahead and work up an outline to share with the team until he had a rough idea how each person was approaching his or her section. It was a classic chicken-and-egg dilemma, and it had become so frustrating that Peter and all his co-workers were blocking.

Blocking Symptoms: Having to work with others in the writing process was making Peter feel like he was chasing his tail. Each time he thought he saw a clear narrative direction ahead, the response he got from the others skewed it in a surprisingly different direction, and he had to go back to the beginning and rethink the entire slant of his work.

As a result, he felt like he'd rather not put anything down on paper until he had some idea what everyone else was doing, so that he could tailor his work in the right direction. Unfortunately, team members felt the same hesitation, so no writing was done at all. The whole project seemed to be disintegrating.

Prescription: OUTLINING, PREFABS, BULLETIN BOARDS. We first told Peter that he should console himself with the fact that the writing process is highly provisional. Until the moment when the last draft is typed up and sent off, all is open to change. So the thing to do is adopt a tentative structure for the proposal, then modify it as the draft evolves and shows you where new alterations are called for. Try a Prefab, we said, if there isn't a standard proposal format for your company, or if a standard format isn't required by your funder. Use the Beginning, Middle, and End, or the Five Ws—Who, What, When, Where, Why. Whatever you select, distribute it to your team, let them know it's provisional, and then sit back and wait for their feedback to indicate how you should tailor the structure to the actual proposal content.

After that, the rest of the process is simple. Display the draft sections so that every contributor has constant access to every other contributor's progress and line of thought as it develops. (Or if a contributor has reached only the notes or lists stages, display index cards with large subject headings corresponding to those on the outline.)

We suggested that Peter find a space that wouldn't be disturbed during the writing process, that he set up large bulletin boards in it, and that he then convene his writing team. When you've discussed the topic and made individual assignments, we said, tell each writer that his or her draft to date will be posted for review by all other members of the team at certain intervals, shorter or longer depending on the deadline pressure (in Peter's case, the interval turned out to be biweekly).

Then schedule group meetings to be held slightly later, so that all team members have an opportunity to look over what everyone else has posted before they come to the group meeting, and are then prepared to raise questions, hash out disagreements, and reach a consensus. Everyone on the team should be made to understand how important it is that he or she attend every meeting.

Finally, we suggested, if the deadline is very tight, set quotas: Each team member must complete so many pages or a certain percentage of his draft section each time a display deadline rolls around. Remember to leave enough time at the end of the writing process for review by all team members, final alterations, and typing.

CASE 4: FEAR OF CRITICISM

Felicia F. is a psychologist. She teaches at a large urban university on the East Coast and works as a consultant to the U.S. Department of Health, Education, and Welfare on occupational health studies. Her specialty is working up incentive programs to persuade industrial workers to comply with government safety and health procedures designed to protect them from industrial accidents and other health hazards.

Felicia is extremely good at delivering short, clear lectures to employees and managers on the importance of health procedures, and she's also a very good writer when it comes to creating simple, directive summations telling workers how to protect themselves.

Felicia came to us for advice because she had just been asked to prepare a research note on her incentive work for the most prestigious journal in her field—one that she'd been unsuccessfully submitting articles to for years—and she was blocking. But her blocking problem was unusual. In fact, we haven't run across another like it in our entire combined teaching and consulting experience.

Blocking Symptoms: Felicia was comfortable with all of the stages of the writing process until she got to the middle of the rough draft. She could prepare and relax effectively, knew her material backward and forward, and was highly motivated to write the article. But when the draft was underway, she began to have problems. She found herself invariably slowing down, and it became harder and harder to keep on writing. Eventually she would stop altogether. Nothing she could do would get the draft going again. All she could do was start over again and write from another, fresher perspective. But that wasn't working—she had tried it a half-dozen times with no luck. The journal's submission deadline was looming, and she was getting desperate.

Prescriptions: GET TO KNOW THE INTERNAL CRITIC, SIGNPOSTS, BREADCRUMBS STRATEGY, REREAD WHAT YOU'VE WRITTEN, CHANGE YOUR TOOLS. Felicia's academic background as a psychologist meant that the concept of an internalized self-critical function was already very familiar to her. We suggested that her tendency to stop in the middle of the process might stem from a fear of the internal critic's admonitions, externalized as a fear of adverse comments from the journal's editorial board. Hearing that interpretation articulated helped Felicia to confront the critic and begin the process of coming to terms with it.

The balance of our advice to her was practical. We described techniques to keep the flow of words coming once she was successfully launched on a rough draft. Felicia was already thoroughly conversant with the concept and practice of rewards, or positive reinforcement, but the obvious simplicity of the Breadcrumbs strategy was a new and valuable concept to her. "Of course," she said when we first described it, "that's why I can't keep the level of my concentration up—I'm too distracted by all those pragmatic reminders of what I need to get at the store and whom I have to call. I'll just start making notes somewhere and go back and collect them later."

Of the other Signposting techniques, Rereading the draft to pick up a sense of its direction and momentum was useful to her, as was our recommendation that she try just Changing Tools once in a while. She was used to writing all her drafts in blue felt-tip, and she found that working directly on the typewriter was a refreshing alternative, as was a fountain pen, black ink, and high-quality parchment bond. "Something about the formality of the ink on the crisp surface makes my thoughts become sharper and more elegant too," she told us.

Finally, we mentioned the value of reminding herself of her own past triumphs when she felt some trepidation about meeting the standards of the journal editors. With renewed insight about the role her internal critic was playing in causing an exaggerated fear of their judgments, Felicia was able to push through her current draft and submit it. It was published a few months later, with exceptionally few revisions.

CASE 5: OVERGENERALIZATION

A public health physician, Georgia J., was having trouble preparing an article on preventive medicine for a popular health magazine. Georgia had struggled through two complete rewrites, taking what she felt were meticulous pains with the piece, but each time it had come back from the magazine's editor with a polite but firm request for further revision: The editor liked the content, but felt that the style was so dull no one would bother reading past the first paragraph. Georgia was so depressed she was just about ready to shelve the entire project, even though she had already invested substantial amounts of time in it.

We weren't sure just what the magazine's editor was objecting to, so we asked Georgia to show us her most recent draft. Here's the first paragraph:

> Rising medical costs are accompanying a decline in the general level of health in this country. This paradox can be resolved only when the medical profession educates the public as to the importance of preventive medicine. A lifetime program of good health habits and a healthy diet would save millions of dollars and produce a healthier population.

Blocking Symptoms: We could understand the editor's objections. The paragraph did sum up the problem in a general way, but it did so in such bland terms that it was lifeless. What, for example, did Georgia mean by "good health habits"? It seemed clear to us that, knowing she was trying to convey complicated material to a very large public audience, Georgia had overgeneralized and thus her material was so abstract as to be boringly trite and self-evident.

Prescription: FRIENDLY EAR, LISTS, OUTLINES, NONSTOPS, READ IT OUT LOUD, REVISER'S TOOLKIT, FOG IN-DEX. Georgia's article was far too vague to attract and hold the attention of a typical magazine reader. Our first suggestion was that she try to make the article livelier and more personal. Didn't she have experiences, anecdotes, and case histories that she could use to flesh out her abstract assertions? Indeed she did, and she repeated to our Friendly Ears tale after tale of patients who had come to her with extensive complaints, all of which a good, thorough program of preventive medicine easily could have averted.

Either capture this material on tape, we said, or jot it down in rough Notes as it comes to you and then pull it together into Lists, simple Outlines, even sections of the rough draft. We recommended that Georgia use one of these stories as a starting place for a Nonstop, letting her unconscious mind dictate what her hand put on paper for a set period of time—five to fifteen minutes. When she reviewed the Nonstop, she'd find that certain concepts, words, and phrases seemed to stand out—these are the essential ingredients of the draft.

When you have the draft pulled together, we said, try Reading It Out Loud to a friend or colleague; there is nothing more valuable for catching your own ambiguities and pomposities than hearing them come out of your own mouth. Finally, we ran through our suggestions for revising and polishing the draft, those that we've included in the Reviser's Toolkit. We reviewed the Fog Index technique and urged Georgia to keep her FI under 10.

Some months later we received a copy of the magazine issue in which Georgia's article had been published, along with a note from her. Our suggestions had worked well for her, she said, and the article was far more interesting:

> Two months ago, a new patient came to see me, a young woman I'll call Terry M. She hadn't been very specific

on the phone about the reason for her visit. When I asked what I could do for her, I was stunned by her reaction: She broke into racking sobs. The week before, she finally managed to tell me, a new checker in the supermarket had mistaken her son for her grandson. Faced with this shocking testimony to her prematurely aged features, Terry had succumbed to a deep depression. She felt homely, undesirable, worthless.

Yet as she sat there in my office, begging me to tell her how to salvage her appearance with pills, injections, surgery—*anything*—some of the causes of her plight were there before me, in plain view. Even as she cried, a cigarette rose from her lap to her mouth with the regularity of a metronome. She was at least 40 pounds overweight. She admitted to drinking "a couple of glasses of wine in the evening" (I had a hunch it might be somewhat more than that, and later tests proved me right). What did she do for exercise? She just shook her head mutely.

I'm afraid my response to Terry's dilemma was somewhat cynical. I've seen too many cases like hers to feel anything but frustration about them. Simple preventive health habits could have saved her from this pain. . . .

10

Personal Writing:

Thank-You Notes, Promotional Features, Personal Letters, Consumer Complaints, Letters to the Editor

OST of this book speaks to those who must write because writing is part of their work or, in the case of student writers, because it's an essential part of the intellectual training process. But nearly all of us, at one time or another, want or need to write for purely personal reasons, and on these occasions anyone can suffer from blocking.

We may want to draft a letter of complaint to the manufacturer or distributor of a defective product we've bought. We may feel the urge to write to the editor of a local paper or the management of a local radio or TV station to express our opinions on a controversial issue. Job or school applications, resumés, and brief personal biographies are common personal writing jobs. Perhaps we simply want to note a few words of greeting, appreciation, or gratitude on a card to a friend. Or we may want to express our feelings to a loved one.

Whatever the occasion, we all find it necessary now and then to put words on paper for personal reasons, and the blocking that we may experience then is no different from the block that inhibits someone who *must* write.

The problem is often the search for a tone of natural genuineness, one that conveys one's thoughts and feelings clearly, fully, accurately. It's never an easy thing to do. You know how you *feel*—if you were standing next to your correspondent, you might want to express yourself by hugging him, or possibly by punching him in the nose—but it's not always clear how to put such feelings into words.

Another way to look at the problem of blocking in personal writing is in terms of assertiveness—the effective balance point between the extremes of aggressiveness on one hand and submissiveness on the other. Submissiveness results from the desire to please and the nagging conviction that your own thoughts, desires, and emotions are not as important as anyone else's. Assertiveness is simply the appropriate, balanced, relaxed, confident expression of a thought or feeling, whether negative or positive. Put succintly, it means being direct and honest, but also tactful and compassionate.

Expressing yourself in this way is never automatic. It must be learned, and just as it can be learned in direct personal interaction with others, so it can also be learned in writing to them.

CASE 1: STRIVING FOR SINCERITY

Three months after her wedding, Janet W. received a call from Aunt Lillian. "Hello, my dear," said the familiar voice at the other end of the line, "this is Lilly. Just calling to say hello and to ask if you actually got the appliquéd bread-warmer that I sent you for the wedding. . . ."

Janet's heart sank. Yes, of course she'd received the breadwarmer, but she hadn't been able to bring herself to sit down and write thank-you notes. She stammered out a lame excuse to Aunt Lilly about having been too busy to write, and made yet another guilty resolution to get those notes written and sent out before she completely lost track of who had given her what.

Blocking Symptoms: Making the resolution was one thing, carrying it out yet another. Every time Janet sat down to write, she'd start by addressing the envelope, begin the note by saying "Thank you for the . . ." and then dry up, unable to think of anything interesting or original to say after that point. The thought of sending out perfunctory, mean-ingless, repetitive messages was so repugnant to her that she couldn't continue. Somehow she couldn't find the inspira-tion she needed. In sum, Janet was afraid of sounding trite, boring, cold, and insincere. So instead of writing, she kept promising herself that she would, but then found endless excuses to put it off.

Prescription: FRIENDLY EAR, PROGRAMMED DAWDLING, TREASURY. Janet had already unknowingly started the process of working on her block when she decided to speak about it to Karin, who encouraged her to continue to talk about it with her family and friends, with anyone who might lend a Friendly Ear.

Reasoning that the most important thing was for Janet not to feel overly pressured or panicked at this point, Karin's second recommendation involved Programmed Dawdling. Since Janet had already spent three unfruitful months trying to get the job done, Karin said, why not just arbitrarily allow herself another three months, if necessary, and do the job right. Janet agreed, and readily conceded that not having the task hanging over her head any longer took a great weight off her shoulders and gave her a crucial sense of liberation about doing it.

Then Karin suggested that since her block seemed to center on her lack of material to write about, Janet needed to develop a wedding gift Treasury file as a source of inspiration. Instead of trying to conjure up fresh, original comments for each gift, while at the same time trying to cope with her guilt feelings about taking so long to write thank-you notes, she should just keep a simple notebook handy to jot down descriptions of every occasion when she actually used something that had been given to her as a wedding gift. This technique wouldn't work for every gift, of course, but Janet found that she used enough of them during just one week so that her notebook was completely filled up.

One typical page looked like this:

(Silver) . . . just gave another dinner party, this time for my boss. Awfully nervous about entertaining him and his wife, but when I set the table with the beautiful silver you sent, the room became completely elegant. Thanks for the props. They helped set the stage for a very important command performance, one in which I performed like a star.

(Coffee maker) . . . it's only the smell of freshly ground coffee that got me out of bed today. We'd been fixing up the apartment until 3:00 in the morning and I just couldn't face going to work. Jim made the coffee before he left—strong, just the way I like it. We thought of you. And will again, every time we use the creative gift you gave us. Thanks.

(Kitchen utensils) . . . we got five of everything we don't need or can't use, but only my practical Aunt Margaret knew that I'd be working in a kitchen and not opening an exotic gift shop. I may not unpack all my crystal goblets for years, but the meals we eat every day couldn't get cooked without your gift.

As you can see, instead of trying to manufacture something that sounded genuine and original about her gifts for every note, Janet let her daily routines offer suggestions and thus expressed something truly personal to her friends and relatives. And within a few weeks, not months, she had written all her thank-you notes and had even enjoyed the process.

CASE 2: SETTING A DAILY QUOTA

Sandy S. is a volunteer who is having trouble meeting a deadline. Her church is holding a fund-raising dinner, with a guest speaker from a nearby university, and she's been asked to write a feature for the local paper to promote the function. But Sandy is blocking.

Blocking Symptoms: Sandy keeps checking her calendar, reducing her estimates of how long it will take her to gather information, write a draft, revise it, and submit it to the paper. She's promised herself over and over again that she'll start the whole process in plenty of time to meet her deadline. But she doesn't. Something ostensibly more urgent always interferes. The days slip by inexorably. Intermediate deadlines come and go, and Sandy jumps nervously each time the phone rings because she knows the next call will be from the paper's editor, a fellow church member, asking more and more urgently when she's going to have the article ready.

Prescription: MAKE WRITING APPOINTMENTS, KEEP A WRITER'S LOG. Once Sandy had agreed that writing this feature was a top priority for her, we recommended that she set up daily quotas—in terms of paragraphs produced—that would bring her to the end of the job by the due date, and that she designate a certain period of the day as her writing time and *stick to it* rigidly, until the job was done.

Then we added a slight twist to this more-or-less standard prescription. We urged Sandy to use any of the writing interval when she wasn't able to work on the feature itself by Keeping a Writer's Log. We felt that she wasn't fully acquainted with her own blocking processes, and that recording her thoughts and impressions about the writing process would help make them plainer to her.

Here's how some excerpts from her journal looked:

RESOLUTION:

> I will spend forty minutes every afternoon working on the article. I will write at least two paragraphs a day. I won't even think about revising until I have completed a rough draft.

FIRST SESSION:

> I sat in front of my typewriter and daydreamed about how good I'll feel when I'm done with this job. But no writing got done.

SECOND SESSION:

> I sat in front of my typewriter for twenty minutes thinking about how lousy I'll feel if I don't do it. Called Marlene, who is in charge of the dinner. After we talked, I listed some of the ideas we thought up.

THIRD SESSION:

> Felt inspired. Came to the typewriter with phrases and sentences running through my head. Got enough done in one session to make up for the two days I wasted.

FOURTH SESSION:

> Reread what I had written, but didn't stop to revise. Finished a first rough draft — but fear it's probably

awful. Will wait until Monday to reread. At least it's done.

FIFTH SESSION:

Turned down a tennis game to stick to the schedule . . . felt very virtuous. The draft isn't all that bad, but there are some soft spots. Made some revising lists, things to remember to check out.

SIXTH SESSION:

The lists worked well—could see just what needed to be done when I reread the thing again. It's coming along fine.

SEVENTH SESSION:

Everyone deserves a day off.

EIGHTH SESSION:

Worked an extra half hour and wrapped the whole job up. Who'd believe it? I did it in small, bite-size chunks, and it's over. I'm even ahead of my schedule. Never would have thought it could happen this way. A good feeling of accomplishment.

As you can see, the log helped Sandy overcome her unconscious hesitation by bringing it to light and helping her see the advantages of writing a little at a time. It also shows how powerful and unpredictable the benefits of writing by a self-imposed schedule can be.

If you're keeping a log as you work, you'll find that the intervals between work sessions will often act as incubating phases, giving you time to digest new material, helping open up your unconscious to new directions and strategies for overcoming difficulties, and allowing you the psychological distance you need to see your work objectively.

CASES 3 AND 4: POWERFUL FEELINGS

Brad N. is an attorney who travels frequently to represent his firm in court appearances in other cities. He has a fiancée,

Linda, whom he met on a vacation trip to Greece some months ago. When Brad first showed up in one of our classes, he confessed that he felt somewhat embarrassed to be there, since his profession required him to write copiously, and he'd never had trouble with writing before in any other context.

But now, when he was away, he suddenly found himself blocking when he tried to write to Linda to tell her of his feelings for her. It wasn't that he couldn't verbalize them; he had no trouble telling her on the phone how he felt, but his personal long-distance phone bills were astronomical. Linda was sending him letters every two or three days that were marvelously expressive, and he wanted to respond in kind, but he couldn't do it comfortably. It might even be, he added, that her ability to communicate her feelings so well was contributing to his block, since although he could write a stunning legal brief, he was uncomfortable and oddly intimidated by his inability to match her passionate eloquence.

At about the same time that we met Brad, another blocking victim came to one of our seminars with a block that also stemmed from the involuntary inhibition of powerful feelings. In Angela T.'s case, the feelings were overwhelmingly negative.

She'd purchased an expensive new car six months before, and since then she'd had nothing but trouble with it. Not only had she undergone endless hassles with the dealer's service department, but the car had developed the nasty habit of breaking down in the most inconvenient places at the worst possible times—such as on the crowded freeway in the middle of the morning commuter rush. Every time Angela tried to talk about how angry she was, her face would flush deeply and she would begin to tremble.

Angela could not write a businesslike, forceful letter of complaint to the dealer and the manufacturer without calming down first. She knew that in her current state of mind, anything she wrote would be so vehement as to sound like the work of a lunatic, and would understandably be ignored by its recipients. So she blocked.

Blocking Symptoms: Both these writers feel uneasy when they have to convey powerful emotion—especially affection or anger—in writing.

When Brad tries to think of something tender and novel to say, his hand cramps up. He becomes depressed. Everything suddenly looks a little flatter and duller, and he feels defeated.

Angela gets agitated. Her blood pressure shoots up. She's so angry about her new car that she can't think calmly enough to state her case well.

Prescription: SYSTEMATIC RELAXATION, KEEP A WRITER'S LOG, GET TO KNOW THE INTERNAL CRITIC, TALK IT INTO A TAPE RECORDER, CRANK LETTER. The essence of these unblocking techniques is acknowledging and articulating strong feelings while staying relaxed enough so that experiencing them doesn't cause renewed tension and blocking. Once you've identified and described to yourself the feelings that are paralyzing you, you can then go on either to bypass them entirely in favor of something more conducive to your goals, or you can work on creatively reshaping them so that they will more successfully help you communicate what you want to express to your reader.

Both Brad and Angela needed to work on Systematic Relaxation before and during the writing process. Brad's cramped hand (the writer's version of tongue-tiedness) and Angela's palpable nervousness were closing down the smooth flow of ideas and phrasings that is essential to effective composition. We summarized the alternative relaxation methods for them and suggested that they choose the one they felt would be most suitable for their lifestyle.

In Brad's case, we suggested Keeping a Writer's Log. In the log he could speak to Linda about the trouble he was having in writing to her, which would give him plenty of material to use later when he wanted to write actual letters to her, since he could make use of the sections that dealt with his feelings. Since Brad was a witty raconteur of self-deprecating anecdotes about the ingenuity of his various blocking strategems, we also suggested that he make the log an oral one by Talking It into a Tape Recorder.

When we saw Brad again, he was very excited. He'd followed our suggestions and found that they worked well for him. He had been able to fill page after page of his letters with amusing stories, and doing so had triggered other associations in his mind about things he wanted to tell Linda. On and on he had written, effortlessly, describing his friends, his colleagues, his daily routines, his thoughts, and, of course, how intensely he missed her. Once Brad had gained confidence in his own personal style, he never again lost touch with it.

In Angela's case, we knew that she was also blocked by strong feelings, but the problem here seemed to be how best to vent and defuse her outrage so that her legitimate complaints wouldn't be dismissed by the car manufacturer as nothing more than hysterical overreaction.

Our first step was to describe the concept of the internal critic to Angela and to explain how the critic induces blocking by inhibiting the writer. In her case, we believed that the critic was acting as a censor and keeping too tight a lid on her boiling fury, giving it no room for expression, thus making it worse and worse. And since her anger was compounded by the critic's repression and by her guilt about feeling so upset, she needed to get in touch with her own self-censoring tendencies in a Crank Letter.

Only when we had convinced Angela that no one would ever read the results was she able to cut loose and write the explosive letter she'd been holding back for months. We couldn't reproduce the unexpurgated version here, but a facsimile goes something like this:

Dear ABC Company:

Your Lion 500 is a lemon. The damn car broke down one day after the warranty expired, and I've spent well over $800 on it since then—all in totally unnecessary expenditures. . . .

I'm ready to take you to court on this one. You can't and won't get away with this crime. The warranty isn't worth the paper it's printed on. . . . No one's reimbursing me for the time I've lost at work and the cost of treating my aggravated ulcer. But I have kept detailed records of repairs I've had to make on this piece of . . . and I intend to get satisfaction for them. You're going to come up with that money, one way or another, and soon! In fact, you'd better prepare to replace this lemon with a new car, if you think you know how to make one that works.

This letter was too heavy-handed to be effective, but it served the purpose of getting Angela's feelings out into the open air. Once she had allowed herself to be thoroughly angry on paper, she could reread what she'd written and reflect more clearly on the content, tone, and purpose of the letter. Then she was able to rewrite it as a forceful but dignified statement to the company on what she had undergone and what she expected them to do about it.

Dear ABC Company:

I am extremely displeased with your product. I bought one of your Lion 500's very recently (see enclosed copy of purchase contract) and in the six months that I have owned it, it has spent more time in the dealer's service shop than on the road—literally. (See enclosed service orders.) Only one day after the limited warranty expired, the car's transmission failed. That was the first of seven major manufacturing or assembling flaws that I have had to contend with. Copies of repair bills and a letter from the

*dealer (confirming my careful maintenance of the car) are
also enclosed.*

*There is quite simply no justification for selling anyone
such a shoddy piece of merchandise. I expect you to extend my
warranty, as well as to reimburse me for all the unnecessary
expenses I have incurred since buying this automobile.*

*Copies of this letter are also being sent to the Consumer
Protection Bureau, to Ralph Nader's organization, and to
my lawyer, who has advised me to consider legal remedies
unless I receive prompt and satisfactory compensation
from you.*

Resolutely,

Angela T.

CASES 5 AND 6: SELF-CONSCIOUS WRITERS

David M., a geologist, had read in local newspapers numerous articles advocating increased oil drilling along the beach
near his home. Now he had heard the same information on
local TV, and the more he heard it, the more concerned he
got—there was no doubt in his mind that the oil companies'
own staff writers were subtly and effectively influencing the
local news media to see things in a too-optimistic light, and a
subtle bias in favor of the drilling program was creeping into
what David felt should be straight news reporting. The
ecologist's side of the story was not being told.

He wanted to help set the record straight by writing
rebuttals to these articles and editorials, but he despaired of
having any effect. When we asked him why he was so
pessimistic about his own powers of expression, he replied
that he simply didn't have the skills and polish that the media
have. "Look," he said, "they're pros. They've been at it for
years. They *know* how to speak to the public and I don't.
How can I compete with that kind of expertise?" So he found
himself blocking. Everything he put on the page sounded

dull, clumsy, and stilted to him. He despaired of ever finding a tone and style that satisfied him and conveyed what he wanted to say.

A similar situation developed with Barbara B., a married student who was on the verge of resigning from the PTA because she felt so embarrassed about the problem her blocking was causing. Barbara had promised to help write the PTA newsletter for the school her kids attended, but then had blocked badly and hadn't been able to cope with it. The deadline had come and gone, and all she had to show for it was a wastebasket full of crumpled papers.

At the heart of Barbara's block, we found, was an extremely strong conviction that because she hadn't written anything but personal letters since her high school English classes, her rusty skills would make her look stupid and expose her family to ridicule. Rather than confront the problem and examine it calmly, she'd been making excuses to the other PTA members, claiming that her kids had been sick, that her husband needed her help, and so on. But the shame and guilt she felt about lying like this to cover up her sense of personal deficiency was only making the block worse.

Blocking Symptoms: If you are like David and Barbara, you feel a strong desire to write, but whenever you sit down at your desk, all you can think about is how clumsy and inept you're going to sound. Reading the fluent prose of professional writers makes you feel hopeless about ever matching their eloquence. And to make matters worse, you imagine them writing effortlessly, confidently, and briskly, as well as movingly. By comparison, you feel totally incompetent, since you have to work so hard just to get a few basic notes down on the page. You're feeling so frustrated that you can't even get started.

Prescription: GET TO KNOW THE INTERNAL CRITIC, CRITICAL READING, CONSTRUCTIVE PLAGIARISM, LETTER TO A

FRIEND, LISTS, NONSTOPS, PROFILE A CRITICAL READER, TALK IT INTO A TAPE RECORDER, REVISER'S TOOLKIT. We first disabused David and Barbara of illusions that (a) they had to equal professional writers in order to perform personal writing tasks well, and (b) professional writers don't have to labor strenuously, and sometimes unsuccessfully, over their work. Look, we told them, this block is just the internal critic speaking. He's exaggerating the competence of other writers, and making you feel more concerned about the quality of your own prose. You need to learn how to take him a lot less seriously, and that means you first have to get to know him better. So we described our Portrayal and Dialogue techniques.

We also urged them to read the newspapers more critically and less credulously, so they could expand their own writing repertoires by taking a close, analytical look at just how professional writers achieve their effects. This critical reading would naturally lead to Constructive Plagiarism as they began to incorporate the same persuasive strategies into their own prose.

Instead of dwelling on his inability to compete with the pros in shaping public opinion, David should try phrasing his rebuttals as though he were writing to a friend, rather than that nameless, faceless entity, The Public. David tried the technique of writing a Letter to a Friend, and here's what resulted:

Dear Fred:

They're at it again. Those greedy corporate SOBs want to drill along the beach two miles down from my place. And have they got the public flummoxed! It's the same place where the landslide last year buried two cars (a fluke no one was killed)—can you imagine what those hills will do in the winter if they've been drilled full of holes? Somewhere there has got to be a state geologist's report on that area, and I intend to find it.

*They say there won't be any accidents. And they'll
keep saying it to us as our houses begin to tilt and slide into
the surf.*

*What are our local officials doing about it? That's
right, you guessed it: nothing. It's scandalous. All that
election talk about conservation and the environment, then
when it comes to a showdown, they wilt like lilies. Or maybe
someone's been getting to them. . . .*

Once he'd started the prose flowing, and some of the
irritation was off his chest, David went back and reread his
diatribe to see if there was anything in it he might be able to
use. Following our advice, he listed the solid points, and
tried the letter over again in a series of Nonstops. As he
worked, he tried to picture the typical reader, someone in his
community who would be likely to pick up a copy of the
paper or watch the local TV news. Writing more coolly and
level-headedly this time, and keeping a typical reader in
focus as he went, he wrote this:

Editor:

*I've had the unpleasant experience in recent weeks of
reading article after article, as well as no fewer than three
separate editorials in your paper, advocating oil drilling
along our local beaches. I'm horrified at the blatant lack of
civic responsibility you and your colleagues in the media are
indulging in. It's easy to parrot the oil companies' lines
about advanced, secure technology, and the need to boost
domestic oil production, but all I can think about are the
serious dangers and unresolved issues that face those who live
in this area.*

*It takes only one major spill to destroy much of the
marine life for generations to come. And what do you intend
to tell someone whose home has disappeared down a hill that
has been weakened because of drilling?*

It seems to me that we should be far more concerned

*with reducing our energy consumption so that we don't have
to continue to pressure one another into taking foolish risks.
It's time to rethink this whole issue and scrutinize the high-
sounding but empty promises made by the oil companies and
their political cronies here. We can't afford to take these
chances. As usual, it's we the people who will pay the bill if
the technologists and entrepreneurs are wrong again.*

Barbara's problem had a slightly different cause. She
was so worried about making a grammatical mistake—
misplacing a comma, choosing a wrong word, using awkward syntax—that she couldn't really concentrate on what
she wanted to say.

We recommended two techniques to Barbara. First, we
gave her a list of simple, straightforward handbooks on
English usage and style and told her to read them over at her
leisure. Second, we suggested that she do Critical Reading to
expose herself to enough well-knit prose so that she could
improve her writing by sheer osmosis. (She told us later that
she found the works by Follett, Bernstein, and Strunk and
White, which we've listed in the bibliography, not only clear
and informative but highly entertaining as well.) Reading
these books made it easier and easier for her to correct her
own grammar and punctuation with confidence.

We also mentioned the advantages of using a tape recorder, not only for collecting ideas and information, but
also for dictating a rough draft. After innumerable frustrating sessions with her typewriter, she broke down, bought a
small, inexpensive tape recorder, and gave the method a try.
The results exceeded our expectations. By talking out her
ideas, Barbara discovered new insights, sharpened her
choice of words, remembered interesting examples and
anecdotes, and came up with new ideas for future newsletter
editions. In short, she became dramatically more spontaneous and creative. Soon the first issue of the newsletter was
written, reproduced, and distributed, and Barbara was bus-
ily at work on the next one.

Bibliography

BUSINESS WRITING

Beeve, Courtland L. *Techniques in Writing: Business Letters, Memos, and Reports*. Sherman Oaks, Calif.: Banner Books, 1978.

Brusaw, Charles T. *The Business Writer's Handbook*. New York: St. Martin's, 1976.

Dodds, Robert H. *Writing for Technical and Business Magazines*. New York: Wiley, 1974.

Ewing, David W. *Writing for Results: In Business, Government, and the Professions*. New York: Wiley, 1974.

Hemphill, Phyllis D. *Business Communications with Writing Improvement Exercises*. Englewood Cliffs, N.J.: Prentice-Hall, 1976.

Ironman, Ralph. *Writing the Executive Report*. New York: Funk and Wagnalls, 1966.

LeFevre, Robert. *Business Research and Report Writing*. New York: McGraw-Hill, 1965.

Parr, William D. *Executive's Guide to Effective Letters and Reports*. Englewood Cliffs, N.J.: Prentice-Hall, 1976.

Sparrow, W. Keats, and Cunningham, Donald H. *The Practical Craft: Readings for Business and Technical Writers*. Boston: Houghton Mifflin, 1978.

Weaver, Robert G., and Weaver, Patricia C. *Persuasive Writing: A Manager's Guide to Effective Letters and Reports*. Riverside, N.J.: Free Press, 1977.

EXERCISE RESOURCES

Bach, Linda. *Awake! Aware! Alive!* New York: Random House, 1973.

Choudhury, Bikram, and Reynolds, Bonnie Jones. *Bikram's Beginning Yoga Classes*. Los Angeles: Tarcher, 1978.

Fraser, Joan. *Relaxercises*. Los Angeles: Pinnacle, 1972.

GENERAL RESOURCES

Allen, Walter. *The Writer on His Art*. London: Pheonix House, 1948.

Bartlett, John. *Bartlett's Familiar Quotations*. 14th ed. Edited by Emily Morison Beck. New York: Little, Brown, 1968.

Bernstein, Theodore M. *The Careful Writer: A Modern Guide to English Usage*. New York: Atheneum, 1973.

Crowley, Malcolm, ed. *Writers at Work: The Paris Review Interviews*. New York: Viking Press, 1959; second series, 1965; third series, 1968; and fourth series, 1976, edited by George Plimpton.

Curme, George O. *A Grammar of the English Language*. 2 vols. Essex, Conn.: Verbatim, 1978.

Flesch, Rudolph. *The Art of Readable Writing*. New York: Collier Books, 1949.

Follett, Wilson. *Modern American Usage: A Guide*. Edited by Jacques Barzun. New York: Hill and Wang, 1966.

Goelber, Carl. *Writing to Communicate*. New York: New American Library, 1974.

Jordan, Lewis, ed. *The New York Times Manual of Style and Usage*. New York: Quadrangle, 1976.

Manual of Style, A. 12th ed. Chicago: University of Chicago Press, 1969.

Strunk, William, Jr., and White, E. B. *The Elements of Style*, 2nd ed. New York: Macmillan, 1972.

Tillett, Nettie S., ed. *How Writers Write.* New York: Thomas Y. Crowell, 1937.

Tripp, Rhoda Thomas. *The International Thesaurus of Quotations.* New York: Thomas Y. Crowell, 1970.

Zinsser, William. *On Writing Well: An Informal Guide to Writing Nonfiction.* New York: Harper & Row, 1976.

PSYCHOLOGY RESOURCES

Adams, James L. *Conceptual Blockbusting: A Pleasurable Guide to Better Problem Solving.* San Francisco: San Francisco Book Co., 1976.

Kubie, L. S. *Neurotic Distortion of the Creative Process.* New York: Farrar, Straus & Giroux, 1961.

Lakein, Alan. *How to Get Control of Your Time and Your Life.* New York: New American Library, 1971.

Progoff, Ira. *At a Journal Workshop: The Basic Text and Guide for Using the Intensive Journal.* New York: Dialogue House, 1975.

Rainer, Tristine. *The New Diary.* Los Angeles: Tarcher, 1978.

Safán-Gerard, Desy. "How to Unblock." *Psychology Today* (January 1978): 78-85.

RELAXATION RESOURCES

Benson, Herbert. *The Relaxation Response.* New York: Avon, 1976.

Tasto, Donald L., and Skjei, Eric W. *Spare the Couch.* Englewood Cliffs, N.J.: Prentice-Hall, 1979.

Werthman, Michael. *Self-Psyching.* Los Angeles: Tarcher, 1978.

STUDENT WRITING

Bernhardt. Bill. *Just Writing*. New York: Teachers and Writers Publications, 1977.

Elbow, Peter. *Writing Without Teachers*. London: Oxford University Press, 1975.

Turabian, Kate L., ed. *Students' Guide to Writing College Papers*. Chicago: University of Chicago Press, 1977.

TECHNICAL WRITING

American Psychological Association. *Publication Manual of the American Psychological Association*. New York: American Psychological Association, 1974.

Barzun, Jacques, and Grace, Henry F. *The Modern Researcher*. New York: Harcourt, Brace, Jovanovich, 1977.

Brogan, John A. *A Clear Technical Writing*. New York: McGraw-Hill, 1973.

Clements, Wallace, and Berlo, Robert C. *The Scientific Report: A Guide for Authors*. Berkeley, Calif.: University of California Press, 1977.

Erhlich, Eugene H. *The Art of Technical Writing: A Manual for Scientists, Engineers, and Students*. New York: Thomas Y. Crowell, 1969.

Foster, John. *Science Writer's Guide*. New York: Columbia University Press, 1963.

Huber, Jack T. *Report Writing in Psychology and Psychiatry*. New York: Harper & Row, 1961.

Johnson, Thomas P. *Analytical Writing: A Handbook for Business and Technical Writers*. New York: Harper & Row, 1966.

Menzel, Donald H.; Jones, Howard M.; and Boyd, Lyle G. *Writing a Technical Paper*. New York: McGraw-Hill, 1961.

Mitchell, John H. *Writing for Technical and Professional Journals*. New York: Wiley, 1968.

Trelease, Sam F. *How to Write Scientific and Technical Papers*. Cambridge, Mass.: M.I.T. Press, 1969.

Index